FLOURISHING TOGETHER

Cultivating a Fruitful Life in Christ

DORINA LAZO GILMORE

Copyright © 2018 Dorina Lazo Gilmore

First printing January 2018

No part of this book may be reproduced or transmitted in any form or by any means electronic or mechanical, including photocopying and recording, or by any information storage or retrieval system, except as may be expressly permitted in writing by the author. Requests should be addressed in writing through www.DorinaGilmore.com.

ISBN-10: 1981645039
ISBN-13: 9781981645039

Book cover and interior designer: Tara Mayberry, TeaBerry Creative
Author photo: Allison Vasquez

Scripture quotations marked (ESV) are from the ESV® Bible (The Holy Bible, English Standard Version®), copyright © 2001 by Crossway, a publishing ministry of Good News Publishers. Used by permission. All rights reserved.

Scripture quotations marked (HCSB) are taken from the Holman Christian Standard Bible®, Copyright © 1999, 2000, 2002, 2003, 2009 by Holman Bible Publishers. Used by permission. Holman Christian Standard Bible®, Holman CSB®, and HCSB® are federally registered trademarks of Holman Bible Publishers.

Scripture quotations marked (NIV) are taken from the HOLY BIBLE, NEW INTERNATIONAL VERSION®, NIV® Copyright © 1973, 1978, 1984, 2011 by Biblica, Inc.® Used by permission. All rights reserved worldwide.

Scripture quotations marked (NLT) are taken from the Holy Bible, New Living Translation, copyright © 1996, 2004, 2007 by Tyndale House Foundation. Used by permission of Tyndale House Publishers, Inc., Carol Stream, Illinois 60188. All rights reserved.

Scripture quotations marked (MSG) are taken from The Message. Copyright © 1993, 1994, 1995, 1996, 2000, 2001, 2002. Used by permission of NavPress Publishing Group.

To order additional copies of this resource, order online through www.dorinagilmore.com.

DORINA LAZO GILMORE is a published writer, blogger, and speaker. Dorina is passionate about helping women from diverse backgrounds flourish in their God-given callings.

Dorina has published three books for children, including the award-winning Cora Cooks Pancit. She has also published a volume of poetry and several chapters in collaborative books. Dorina shares her words around the inter-webs at places such as (in)Courage, For Every Mom, Kindred Mom, In All Things, and on her personal blogs www.DorinaGilmore.com and www.DorinaKidsBooks.com.

Dorina is married to Shawn, and a mama to three active girls. When she isn't taxi driving her girls to school and activities, Dorina loves to run marathons, visit the ocean, curl up with a book, or gather people around her table for a good meal.

Learn more about Dorina's work and join her Glorygram list at www.DorinaGilmore.com.

Use the hashtag #FlourishingTogether on social media to share about this study and connect with others on the journey.

Updated © January 2018 Dorina Lazo Gilmore-Young
No part of this Booklet may be reproduced in any way.

*For my husband, Shawn,
who continues to teach me the
value of rest and
encourages me to
flourish in my calling.*

CONTENTS

Introduction 1

ONE — Plant 11

TWO — Prune 27

THREE — Rest 47

FOUR — Nourish 65

FIVE — Cultivate 83

SIX — Bloom 99

Dear Leader Friends 115

End Notes... 117

Acknowledgements 123

INTRODUCTION

For me, 2016 started with an unexpected and bountiful harvest. On January 16, Shawn and I celebrated our wedding—a true redemption story after losing my beloved Ericlee to cancer in 2014. That year was a journey of finding God's glory even in the darkest hours. Then 2015 was a year to redeem, to witness God bringing new value to all that had been broken and lost for our family. As I stood at the altar with my bridegroom, surrounded by more than 500 friends and family, I felt like I was being **planted** in a new and spacious garden. I was eager to flourish.

I chose "flourish" as my focus word for 2016. At the start, flourish sang to me of bright colors and new beginnings. The dictionary says "flourish" is a verb, meaning to thrive; to grow luxuriantly; to be in one's prime; to be at the height of fame, influence, success; to prosper.[1] It is with this that I marched into 2016 with a spirit of newfound joy and fierce hope.

Andy Crouch writes this in his book *Strong and Weak*, "To flourish is to be fully alive, and when we read or hear those words something in us wakes up, sits up a bit straighter, leans ever so slightly forward. To be fully alive would connect us not just to our own proper human purpose but to the very heights and depths of divine glory."[2]

Of course, just as in past years, I had no idea how that one word would shape me, challenge me, break me and remake me from the inside out.

INTRODUCTION

A few months into 2016, I started to feel overwhelmed. I had way too much on my plate. I was still leading in several large capacities, while adding a new husband, a new family situation and a giant new speaking/writing project to my list. Something had to give. In a conversation on one of our regular date nights, my hubby gently suggested I clear my plate of commitments so I could really focus on the new projects God was calling me to. I balked.

Clear everything from my plate at one time? Who does that? I loved everything I was involved in. Every piece felt important and meaningful. What could I possibly cut back or step down from? They needed me, right? I hemmed and hawed. I strategized about ways I could keep certain things and be more efficient with my time.

One afternoon, I overheard my mother-in-law giving my middle daughter a lesson in keeping roses. The two of them were on the front patio of our new home with huge garden clippers. I saw the sad state of our rose bushes. The one in the middle had two thick, root branches that were so heavy they were making the whole bush topple forward. As Grandma directed, my 7-year-old went to work pruning branches. Even some of the prettiest roses on the bush had to be clipped for the good of the entire bush.

The lesson was not lost on me. I knew deep in my heart it was time to **prune**.

These familiar words echoed in my heart: "I am the true vine, and my Father is the vinedresser. Every branch in me that does not bear fruit he takes away, and every branch that does bear fruit he prunes that it may bear more fruit." (John 15: 2-3).[3]

Did you catch that? It doesn't say he leaves the branches that are thriving, the biggest branches, the ministries that look the most successful, and the activities that bring in the most people or seem to depend the most on you. The verse says every branch—even the ones bearing fruit—must be pruned.

Hadn't I already learned enough about pruning? After all, in the past year and a half I had surrendered my husband to cancer, my position helping lead a non-profit in Haiti, several circles of friends and so many of my lifelong dreams for our family. Letting go of those things was excruciating. Why would God ask me to give up more?

He was asking me to be obedient. I now know He wanted me to let go of some good things that had become so big in my life that they had begun to define me. These were the thickest branches of my rose bush weighing me down. He wanted me to lean into His present calling on my life to allow my identity to be re-defined in Him.

That spring I stepped down from my teaching job at the university. I prayed for another mama leader to take on my role leading a thriving moms' group at our church. God answered my prayer and raised up another woman from my leadership team to be the coordinator. I stepped out of some other community groups and declined invitations to speak and attend events that were regular on my calendar through the years.

At first, it was much harder than I thought it would be. I thought I could just move on to the next thing, but I discovered that even when God prunes us for the good, we need to give ourselves time to grieve. I missed the communities and circles of friends. I missed the sense of purpose I had felt in those spaces. I felt restless and alone. I wanted to rest, but I discovered something scary about myself. I didn't know how to **rest**.

After operating a non-profit more than a decade with my husband and working in highly-demanding leadership and ministry places, I didn't know how to sit in the quiet. In those months of pruning, my branches felt naked and bare, with no sign of green or color. I had to learn to wait and listen and trust God.

During the summer of that year, I chose to focus on a few things to nourish my soul and my body. I chose to read more books and signed up to run a full marathon. These were significant and intentional choices not to merely fill my time, but to learn to be quiet and enjoy solitude. As I logged several hundred miles, I started to feel alive again. Running provided concentrated time to listen and to pour out my heart to God. When I would come home from long runs, I was exhausted and ready to rest. Naps were unapologetically part of my day.

One day, Jesus said to the Samaritan woman at the well, "Everyone who drinks of this water will be thirsty again, but whoever drinks of the water that I will give him will never be thirsty again. (John 4:13-14).[4] Like my thirsty rose bushes, my soul needed, and continues to need, water. I needed to let this living water seep deep into my soul soil and **nourish** my roots. For years, I had only afforded myself quick drinks at the drinking fountain. This summer, I drank deeply from the well. I gave myself permission to rest, to run with my Father and to spend time investing in my husband and daughters. That nourishing phase was important to help me recalibrate my heart and for all of us to bond as a family.

When September rolled around, our family rhythm changed again. My girls went back to school, and for the first time in more than a decade, I had at least three full days a week to focus on my writing. I had dreamed of having this time for years, and it was finally here. It felt revolutionary somehow. I had time to work on editing and sending out several of the children's book manuscripts I had written. I also had a little more mental space to work on a bigger book and a Bible study project.

One day as I was slipping in our front door, the rose bushes in front of our door snagged my attention. Huge pink blooms the size of my 5-year-old's head were budding on multiple branches. I had never seen roses this big. We clipped half a dozen to put in the huge, glass vase on our dining room table—a reminder that God often allows us to bloom in unexpected ways in His perfect timing. These gargantuan blooms were the result of the pruning my daughter and mother-in-law had done earlier that year.

In November, I received an email from a children's book agent that she was interested in representing my work. Then I heard from two other agents. After 10 years of receiving rejection letters and wading through the discouragement of having little time to devote to my writing, I had choices. Multiple agents were interested in my work. It was a glimmer of hope. For such a time as this, the Lord had brought me into a season of **cultivating** my writing career and sharing my stories for His glory.

That fall, my husband Shawn and I prayed for the opportunity to develop relationships with more families from our daughters' school. We signed up to help coach the cross country team. We decided this was something we could invest in as a family. Just before Christmas, we hosted an end-of-season celebration at our house. As kids jumped on the trampoline in the yard, and the kitchen and dining room were spilling with parents and coaches, I felt a deep joy welling up inside. I flushed with the color of this new garden in which we found ourselves **blooming**.

If I had not gone through the process of planting, pruning, resting, nourishing, and cultivating, I might not have the chance to experience these surprising blooms.

One of the important lessons I learned this year is that flourishing does not happen in isolation. Flourishing happens together in community. Author and Bible study teacher Margaret Feinberg speaks to this in her book *Flourish*: "We are to help others flourish as we do the same. Electrifying the dreams of others energizes our own God-given dreams."[5] Flourishing together is our highest calling and our greatest opportunity to participate in the glory of God.

Tonight I return to the words of John 15:8: "By this my Father is glorified, that you bear much fruit and so prove to be my disciples."[6]

INTRODUCTION

In a year's time, God has taught me much about the *process of flourishing*. I cannot become a flourishing garden overnight. In fact, I have to consider how to plant and root myself in good soil. I have to prepare myself to be pruned in every area at one time or another. I need to set aside time for rest and nourishment. Most importantly, I need to cultivate my time, my talents, and my privileges so those around me bloom as well.

The goal of this study is to explore this process. Together we will look for flourishing imagery and metaphors used throughout the Bible. We will follow the stories of key Bible characters, including Joseph, Mary Magdalene, Esther, Rahab and Paul, who learned to flourish by trusting the hands of the Master Gardener and leveraging their privileges for others. Grab your gardening tools, a journal, and your Bible, and join me for this season of **flourishing together.**

How to Study

If you are new to studying the Bible, welcome! This will be a grand treasure hunt for you if you put in the time and allow the Holy Spirit to guide you. If you have studied God's Word for many years, my prayer is that this Bible study will open your mind and heart to new truths and give you a different perspective on your own circumstances. At the core of this study is an invitation to dive into God's Word, which I believe is living and applicable for all of our lives today. Isaiah 55:11 says, "It is the same with my word. I send it out, and it always produces fruit. It will accomplish all I want it to, and it will prosper everywhere I send it." (New Living Translation).

If you are new to the Bible stories mentioned in these pages, I want to encourage you to read the entire story, not just isolated verses. For a quick overview, you might consider reading the stories in a children's Bible. Some of my favorites include: *The Jesus Storybook Bible* by Sally Lloyd-Jones or *The Complete Illustrated Children's Bible* by Janice Emmerson, to name a few. These give a window into the stories and are easily digestible in a short amount of time.

In this study, I sometimes encourage you to look up verses or passages in different translations of the Bible. There are many ways to do this, such as using web sites like www.biblestudytools.com or www.biblehub.com. I also like to use the YouVersion bible app on my devices. They include a number of different translations for comparison. You can also use these same tools if you are doing a word study. Maybe there is one theme or word you would like a definition for or would like to see how it is used in context in the Bible. You might look in the Strong's Bible concordance offered in print or online. Strong's includes Hebrew and Greek translation so readers can explore the original languages of the Bible.

I encourage you to explore some of these tools on your own as a way to dig deeper into God's Word. The ultimate goal is to help you understand what is happening in the text of the Bible and to apply God's Word to your life today.

INTRODUCTION

Music Playlist

This study is designed to be interactive on many levels. My hope is that you will engage in God's Word and worship in some new ways through this study. I believe music is one way that we can deepen our understanding of the Bible and feel God's presence. I curated a playlist of worship music to accompany our Flourishing Together Bible study. Each song is connected to the theme of flourishing and the lessons throughout this workbook.

To access the playlist, you can follow my "Flourishing Together" playlist on the free program/app called Spotify or download these songs to your smart phone, computer or other device. You might choose to dig deeper by looking up the lyrics to the songs and treat them as supplementary reading. Steep yourself in this music as you study. See what God reveals.

"For Your Splendor" by Christy Nockels—Into the Glorious

"Garden" (Live) by Matt Maher—Saints and Sinners

"Flourishing" (Psalm 119) by Sandra McCracken—Psalms

"Beautiful Things" by Gungor—Beautiful Things

"Out of Dry Ground" by Austin Stone Worship—The Reveille, Vol. 2

"Closer" by Lifepoint Worship—Victorious

"Desert Song—Live" by Hillsong United—Across the Earth: Tear Down The Walls

"Thrive" by Casting Crowns—Thrive

"Psalm 116 (You Turned My Soul To Rest)" by Robbie Seay Band—Psalms LP

"Tall Cedars" by Austin Stone Worship—The Reveille, Vol. 1: Instrumental

"Into the Deep (Live) by Citipointe Live—Into the Deep

"Breathe" by Jonny Diaz—Everything is Changing

"Rest in You" by All Sons & Daughters—Rest in You

"Daily Bread" by Strahan—Posters

"Living Water" by Ellie Holcomb—Red Sea Road

"Beautiful Scandalous Night" by Robbie Seay Band—Raise Up the Crown

"On the Third Day" by Bethany Dillon—In Christ Alone—Modern Hymns

"Water to Wine" by Hillsong United—Wonder

"Cecie's Lullaby" by Steffany Gretzinger—The Undoing

"All Is Not Lost" by The Brilliance—All Is Not Lost

"Psalm 23 (Live)" by Shane & Shane—Psalms Live

"On The Way" by Elizabeth Hunnicutt—On The Way

"You are the Sun" by Sara Groves—Add To the Beauty

"Rain/Reign" by Hillsong United—Wonder

"The Garden" by Kari Jobe—The Garden

"Seasons Change (Live)" by United Pursuit, Michael Ketterer—Simple Gospel

"Little Things With Great Love (Live)" by The Porter's Gate, Madison Cunningham—Work Songs

"The Secret Place" by Phil Wickham—Children of God Acoustic Sessions

WEEK ONE
PLANT

During the long days and months following my husband's funeral, I began to take inventory of my life. Everything looked dead, dry and malnourished. I felt like a shriveled, thirsty plant, grieving my past and uncertain about my future. I had experienced life in a flourishing garden, but suddenly I felt uprooted and alone. Once confident and courageous, I was suddenly unsure of myself, my decisions, my parenting—everything. If you have ever left a home, a church, or a job, lost a loved one, suffered a health condition or watched a dream die, perhaps you can relate.

I needed God to do a new thing in me. After losing my husband, I was tempted to doubt, but I had evidence that God was faithful. He carried our family through my husband's sickness and death. He provided for every one of our needs. I had three daughters who were also looking to their mama to help them navigate the grief journey. My deepest desire was to live out my husband's legacy of faith. I needed to give myself permission to grieve and also to step forward in hope.

God's promise expressed in Isaiah 43:19 provided that glimmer of hope for my weary soul: "Behold, I am doing a new thing; now it springs forth; do you not perceive it? I will make a way in the wilderness and rivers in the desert."[7] I love the way this scripture starts with the word "behold." Behold is a word that serves as a reminder to pause, to *be held* by my heavenly Father and to marvel at His work. I made that verse my personal theme for that season.

I felt God calling me to return to the seed of my faith, the foundation of the Gospel message. When a seed is planted, it is intentionally placed in the ground. The seed is buried in the soil, and this is the beginning of a plant's life cycle. The seed needs water, light, and oxygen to grow. If the seed has these, it will begin to break open exposing the soft flesh of its insides. The seed dies in the breaking open, and then true growth begins.

Out of the brokenness comes abundance. Out of death comes new life. This, of course, is the crux of the Gospel message. Jesus was the seed planted by God. He suffered and died, was buried in the ground, and emerged a resurrected man. He sacrificed his life so we might flourish. Ann Voskamp, author of the *The Broken Way*, writes, "There is no growth without change, no change without surrender, no surrender without wound—no abundance without breaking. Wounds are what break open the soul to plant the seeds of a deeper growth."[8] I knew I was wounded and broken, but I longed for new life. I prayed for God to use my brokenness and my story for His glory.

A dear friend of mine shared this vision with me. She said she saw two trees planted side by side. Both were well-watered and flourishing with robust branches and lush leaves. As she watched, one of the trees began to struggle. The once-strong branches were falling from the tree. The trunk wavered, and the tree eventually shrunk back and died. The other tree wept at the loss of her companion. She felt alone in the forest.

Then something extraordinary happened. My friend saw all the nutrients from the dead tree enriching the soil and nourishing the living tree. The tree's roots went deep and her trunk grew strong. Her branches stretched farther and longer than they had before. Flowers began to bloom on the tree as she flourished in a new way.

My friend believed the first tree was my husband—a pillar of faith, a leader full of passion and charisma, who God called home. The other tree was me. She believed God would grow a ministry through my story. She spoke these prophetic and encouraging words to me at a time when I wondered if I ever might flourish again without my beloved. That picture of the two trees reached into my heart and gave me hope for the future. I prayed for God to plant me, to root me, and to make a way.

Let's consider together what it means to be planted or rooted in Christ. In this week's homework, you will be digging into several Old Testament and New Testament examples of flourishing. Perhaps my favorite example is in Jeremiah 17:7-8: "But blessed are those who trust in the LORD and have made the LORD their hope and confidence. They are like trees planted along a riverbank, with roots that reach deep into the water. Such trees are not bothered by the heat or worried by long months of drought. Their leaves stay green, and they never stop producing fruit."[9] These verses contain some important clues for us about what flourishing looks like.

First, this passage describes trees planted near the river with roots that reach deep into the water. I noticed the roots do not wait for the water to come to them. They actually chase after the water source. They are intentional to reach deep just as we need to reach out for God if we want to flourish. In John 7:38, Jesus shares these words: "If anyone thirsts, let him come to me and drink."[10] Jesus invites us to reach out to Him, to be rooted in Him.

The root is a vital organ of the plant, which performs several key functions for plant growth. The root allows nutrients from water to enter the plant and be transported to other parts of the plant. The roots also function as a kind of anchor in the ground for the plant as it grows. Roots serve as a storage for food and nutrients the plant needs.[11] When we are rooted in Christ, he connects us to the nutrients we need. He builds us up with truth. He infuses us with love, joy, peace, patience, kindness, gentleness and self-control—beyond what we have on our own.

In the Jeremiah passage, the flourishing trees are the ones that do not fear the heat or drought. Once we are rooted in Christ, we do not need to fear the present or the future. He anchors us with His presence and provides stability even in trials. We can continue to return to Christ for the nourishment and the food we need.

The roots of a plant grow underground. We might compare this to our private life with Christ. If we want strong roots, we need to grow a personal relationship with God. This happens by spending time alone with Him. We can connect with Him through prayer, reading the Bible, and various forms of worship. The important work happens underground when no one else is watching.

> **Seeds of Truth:**
> *"Don't dig up in doubt what you planted in faith."*
> —Elisabeth Elliot

While roots grow underground, the stem of a plant or trunk of a tree grows upward above the ground. The leaves and the fruit serve as visual evidence that a plant or tree is flourishing. We might compare this to our public or community life. When we are rooted deeply in Christ and have an understanding of grace, we desire to reach out and invest in others. We cannot truly flourish alone because God has designed us for community. God calls us to flourish together in the larger garden of His Kingdom. We have specific work we are called to live out in community.

In his letter to the Ephesians, the apostle Paul reminds them of their roots in the faith. "God saved you by his grace when you believed. And you can't take credit for this; it is a gift from God. Salvation is not a reward for the good things we have done, so none of us can boast about it. For we are God's masterpiece. He has created us anew in Christ Jesus, so we can do the good things he planned for us long ago."[12] Paul articulates well that we are saved by grace when we believe. Like the seed, we are made new when the water and nutrients enter in. Then we begin to grow roots downward and bear fruit upward. This is part of God's plan for us.

The flourishing trees described in Jeremiah 17: 7-8 have leaves that stay green and never stop producing fruit. This is a call to believers of all ages. We are never too young or too old to bear fruit. God wants all of us to experience His abundance by flourishing together. He brings beauty from our brokenness when we share our stories and bear each other's burdens.

I experienced this in a profound way. In my grief journey, I had to root myself anew in Christ without my husband and depend on my Maker to be my Provider. Although I was broken, I believed God could nourish my family and bring new life. I just didn't know exactly what it would be like. God grew courage and faith in me in a season of waiting and dependence. This was the work He was doing underground.

Eventually, God brought my new husband Shawn. He was a close friend to my late husband Ericlee. They used to run races and attend church together. I met Shawn on the same mission trip when I met Ericlee in 2001. Shawn was my prayer partner and we coached together. Through the years, Ericlee and I often prayed for Shawn's future wife even trying to set him up with our single friends. I never imagined God was saving Shawn to one day redeem our family and our loss. God planted Shawn in our garden. His presence brought new life out of the tragic death of my first husband. He became a new daddy for my daughters. As a new family, we are now experiencing the growth and abundance that comes from being planted by Christ.

> **Meditate & Memorize:**
> *"But blessed are those who trust in the LORD and have made the LORD their hope and confidence. They are like trees planted along a riverbank, with roots that reach deep into the water. Such trees are not bothered by the heat or worried by long months of drought. Their leaves stay green, and they never stop producing fruit."*
> —Jeremiah 17:7-8[13]

PLANT

DAY ONE

1. Look up the word "flourish" in a few dictionaries. (For example, you might look in the Webster-Merriam's dictionary, a Bible dictionary like Logos, or a web site like BibleStudyTools.com.) Write down a few of the definitions from each that you find interesting. What does it mean to flourish?

   Grow or a develop in a healthy or vigorous way

2. Complete this statement: When I think of something flourishing, I think of *roses blossoming*

   I think of pruning and cutting away dead/old to make way for new

3. Sketch or draw something flourishing below. Not an artist? Don't worry. Look up some images on the internet that represent flourishing. Print one out to share or paste here.

DAY TWO

Today we are going to move on to an Old Testament example of flourishing mentioned in the introduction to this section. In this passage, the prophet Jeremiah is speaking to the people of Judah—primarily those living in Jerusalem as well as those who had already been deported to Babylon. Jeremiah uses tree imagery throughout his prophecy. In chapter 17, he is talking about the sin and punishment of Judah.

4. Read Jeremiah 17. Jeremiah illuminates a contrast between two types of trees in verses 5-8. What characterized the trees in the desert?

   5 bush in wastelands - not see prosperity
   8 tree planted by water that sends its roots out to the streams.

5. What characterized the flourishing trees?

   Never fails to bear fruit, has deep roots and is planted by water that enriches it.

6. What does this chapter reveal to you about what flourishing looks like?

   God searches heart, examines the mind —
   blessed is the one who trusts in the Lord

7. Do you feel like you are surviving or flourishing in your life right now? Explain.

I feel like flourishing. Like everything has been planted and I must bear fruit of the good seed planted in me.

Because of Christ we are able to step into a life of abundance and flourishing. In John 7:37-38, Jesus shares these words, "Let anyone who is thirsty come to me and drink. Whoever believes in me, as Scripture has said, rivers of living water will flow from within them." Meditate on these words today.

Let anyone who is thirsty come to me and drink.

Rivers of living water will flow.

DAY THREE

The Psalms were written mostly by Israel's King David. One of the unique parts of the Psalms is the way David expresses highs and lows. He pours out his emotions to his Father and we get to witness that exchange. God called David a man after his own heart. He was rooted in his relationship with God evidenced in the depth of his interaction with God. The Psalms remind us that flourishing is a reflection of where our hearts are regardless of where we are physically.

8. Psalm 1 is the introduction to the book and considered to be a "wisdom Psalm," offering advice for fruitful living. The words paint a contrast between the righteous and the wicked. Bearing this in mind, read Psalm 1 in two different versions of the Bible. Write down which versions you read. What do you learn about flourishing from this Psalm?

    NIV + The Message
    This about difference; dichotomy - difference of wicked and righteous and God pulling us toward righteousness

9. In verse 2, it talks about meditating day and night on the law of the LORD. The word "meditate" suggests pondering something, reading aloud for personal edification, or reciting memorized passages. What does this say to you about flourishing?

    That by reading the Bible often we are taking in life and finding a way to flourish.

10. What is significant about the tree planted near streams of water?

It is flourishing at the living water — the stream is necessary for its aliveness.

11. How are the images used in Psalm 1 similar to/different from the flourishing images described in Jeremiah 17 from yesterday's reading?

Very similar in comparison of what dies and what is abundant.

12. What is your takeaway from this Psalm?

Meditating and taking in the living water leads to life.

DAY FOUR

Today we are going to take a look at a different Psalm later in the collection that includes flourishing imagery. Psalm 92 is considered a song of thanksgiving, offering praise to Yahweh as King. This psalm was a song for the Sabbath Day and specifically talks about the themes of God's love and faithfulness. Read Psalm 92 in the English Standard Version of the Bible.

13. What are some of the flourishing images or words you find in this Psalm?

    Evildoers flourish but will be destroyed. Righteous flourish in house of God. Stay fresh and green

14. Read verses 12-15 again. What are the righteous compared to in this passage?

    Palm tree that bears fruit.

15. Where should the righteous be planted according to verse 13? What does that look like for you today?

    In the house of God

16. In verse 14, it talks about bearing fruit in old age. Why is this important if we are living to flourish together?

All the days of life they will bear fruit.

17. Write out a verse from this Psalm that spoke to you. How does this verse encourage you to flourish today?

Good people will prosper like palm trees, Grow tall like Lebanon cedars; transplanted to God's courtyard. They'll grow tall in the presence of God, lithe & green, virile still in old age.

My mountain, my huge holy mountain

DAY FIVE

Today we are going to dig into a New Testament example of flourishing. Jesus was a storyteller. He made his teaching relatable and often used examples from daily life and nature. He told Parables, which were earthly stories with heavenly meaning, to teach a given lesson. The details were not as important as the lesson Jesus conveyed through the Parable. In Matthew 13, Jesus tells the Parable of the Sower. Let's dig into the story together.

18. Read Matthew 13:1-23. What are the types of soil described in this story?

   path, rocky place, thorns, good soil

19. How would you describe your heart today? Which soil can you relate to and why?

   There have been times I heard through path, rocky or thorns, but it is the good soil that takes root and pulls me back consistently

20. Matthew 13:18-23 gives the interpretation of this parable. After reading this section, how would you describe what it means to be sown on good ground or in good soil?

It means of having roots to listen and really discern, understand deeply in my heart.

21. What are some ways you are feeling called to seek the Sower (God) and be rooted in good soil today?

To inspire, reach others through who I am in Christ — shining light that cannot be dimmed.

DAY SIX

22. Take some time to observe a plant, a tree or a flower in your environment. Jot down some things you notice about that example of life. Notice the soil, the trunk, the roots, the leaves, the petals, the colors and shapes. Dare to get your hands dirty. Breathe in the aroma. Write a description of what you experience or draw a picture. How does this plant speak to you about flourishing?

A new plant with roots that dig deep drinking in water for nourishment. Taking hold of deep, rich soil and shooting forth with lush greenery to signify hope and new life.

23. Write out a prayer to God about flourishing in this season. Ask him to prepare the soil for you and root you deeply as you study His word in the weeks to come.

O God, I see the way You have me flourishing in this world. Help me to shine my light brightly and bring love and inspiration — through You and for your glory.

WEEK TWO
PRUNE

I gathered a group of seven friends at my dining room table for lunch. We are all leaders who serve at churches and in ministries across the city. These women challenge me, pray over me, and inspire me daily with their courage and vulnerability. I placed a small bouquet of barely-opened daffodils tied with a ribbon at each of their plates. I encouraged my friends to take their daffodils and put them in water as a reminder to "Bloom where you are planted."

A few days later, I started getting text messages from my friends—pictures of their lemon yellow flowers blooming. One friend put hers in a mason jar. Another added hers to a vase tied with raffia. A third used her daffodils to dress up her table's centerpiece and added greenery.

The final photo I received was of a bud vase stuffed full with daffodils. The flowers were limp, shriveled at the ends, floundering. My friend sent the following text to all of us with her photo: "Life lesson: Don't stifle your growth by putting yourself or your dreams in a too-small vase."

The visual was profound for all of us. I was in a season where I heard God whispering that I needed to step back. I needed to create margin for myself. I found myself in a new marriage and a new family dynamic after the death of my first husband. I needed to devote more time to my three daughters. I wanted to spend quality time with my new husband establishing our relationship. I also saw that God was beginning to use my story of tragedy and triumph to encourage others. I couldn't step into that calling unless I carved out the necessary time to pursue it.

My new husband gently and wisely told me: "If you don't say no to some commitments now, you will not have space in the future to step into the big things I believe God is calling you to."

I hemmed. I hawed. I squirmed at his words.

I knew he was right. His voice resonated with what God was already telling me. If I really wanted to flourish in my calling, I needed to prune back some of the big commitments in my life—even the things I loved. This was about obedience to God's nudging.

I took my own bundle of daffodils and put them in the biggest, widest glass vase I could find—a wedding gift from a mentor-friend. That vase—full of water and space and vibrant, yellow flowers—served as a daily reminder to me about what I need to flourish: space to hear God, space to grow, space to add new and different flowers when the time arises.

In John 15, beginning in verse 4, Jesus unfolds a powerful analogy of a vine and branches. He describes two kinds of branches: one that remains in the vine and bears fruit and one that does not remain in the vine and is burned. The Message version of the Bible illuminates this passage:

Live in me. Make your home in me just as I do in you. In the same way that a branch can't bear grapes by itself but only by being joined to the vine, you can't bear fruit unless you are joined with me. I am the Vine, you are the branches. When you're joined with me and I with you, the relation intimate and organic, the harvest is sure to be abundant. Separated, you can't produce a thing.[14]

That phrase "make your home in me" jumped off the page as I read it. Just a chapter earlier Jesus was talking about dwelling together in His Father's house and going to prepare a room for us. What does it mean for us to make our home in Jesus? What do I need to let go of so I have time to be joined with Jesus every day? What do I need to cut away in my life so my eyes are focused like a laser beam on God's purpose for me?

David Roper reflects on this passage in his devotional book, *A Burden Shared*. He writes:

> Sometimes, it seems, we too have to be cut back, almost to nothing. It isn't always the dead and ugly branches that have to go either (we're glad to be rid of those), but the living and vital must be put to death that a better and more bountiful thing may grow...But the knife that cuts is in fact a pruning knife, putting an end to our life so that in the end we may be what we ought to be—living memorials of Jesus.[15]

Of course, as Roper describes, pruning is not just about cutting off the dead, sinful branches. Jesus says *all* branches must be pruned—even the living and vital branches. The process of pruning is painful. For me, some of the largest, heaviest branches had to be pruned back so I had space to abide in the Vine. Prune means "to cleanse, trim, purge, cut away, remove the superfluous or unwanted parts."[16] The hardest part of the process for me was determining what needed to be cut back. I had to open my hands before the Father, the Vinedresser, and ask Him if there was anything that needed to be cleansed or removed so I could live wholly for His glory. The old life and way of doing things needed to be put to death so I could live with new growth.

I heard Him specifically ask me to step down from leading the MOPS group at our church and from teaching at the university. Admittedly, it was difficult to let go. Leading moms at MOPS and teaching were central parts of my life for more than a decade. My identity was defined by these positions. I thrived on the success tasted and the influence I had there. I believed this is part of the reason God wanted to prune me. I was investing so much in those positions that my family was suffering, and I had no space for His best for me.

I also had to lay down my pride. I am a high-capacity, "yes" person, who loves to multi-task. My to-do list is always a mile long. I love to be involved in a lot of different areas, and I feel loyal to a lot of groups of people. If I could keep all the plates spinning, then I felt accomplished. I felt strong and brave. Through the season of pruning, God began to teach me that sometimes I need to be a "no" person for the sake of my family and my calling. I don't need to fill every square on the calendar. I need emotional space to breathe and abide in Him.

In a culture that places a high value on efficiency and high capacity, God wanted me to be counter-cultural. He wanted me to choose margin. He prompted me that this was the time to pass the torch to other leaders he had carefully selected. My role could be to empower them and transition them well. He was urging me to bring out the larger vase with less flowers and more space to bloom.

I recognize that not everyone might be called to prune their lives in the way God pruned me. There isn't a certain formula. He calls us to abide in Him, which requires spending time with Him, listening and following where He leads us. This is part of the flourishing process. Andy Crouch writes this about flourishing: "Here's the paradox: flourishing comes from being both strong and weak. Flourishing requires us to embrace both authority and vulnerability, both capacity and frailty—even at last in this broken world, both life and death."[17] I found myself standing right in the middle of that paradox. The pruning process requires vulnerability. It exposes our weaknesses, the things that distract us from abiding, and the idols we elevate above our identity in Christ. It takes strength to step into the pruning process and to surrender control to the Master Gardener who sees the big picture of His garden.

> **Seeds of Truth:**
> *"Sometimes when you're in a dark place you think you've been buried, but actually you've been planted."*
> – Christine Caine

"But the pruning knife is guided by a pair of good hands," explains David Roper. "The vinedresser…dreams of what we can become—more loving, joyful, tranquil, tolerant, kindly, dependable, gentle, poised, and strong."[18] I don't know about you, but I long for that. I'd much rather reap that kind of harvest than be patting myself on the back for keeping a mess of plates spinning.

My challenge for you this week is to press in for the pruning. As you prepare each day to study John 15 and the story of Joseph, begin by opening your hands and asking God to clearly reveal to you His will through these scriptures. Start to pray about what God wants you to prune from your life.

Have courage, and pass Him the scalpel so He can begin the heart work.

> **Meditate & Memorize:**
>
> *"I am the true vine, and my Father is the vinedresser. Every branch in me that does not bear fruit he takes away, and every branch that does bear fruit he prunes, that it may bear more fruit."*
>
> —John 15: 1-2[19]

DAY ONE

The book of John was written by the Apostle John, brother of James and son of Zebedee. John was likely writing for the Christians who lived in Asia Minor, but the text indicates that he was truly writing for both Christians and non-Christians. The theme of the book is that readers might believe Jesus is the Messiah, the Son of God. He quotes Jesus unpacking seven "I am" statements in the book. John 15 is the seventh and final statement.[20]

1. Read John 15: 1-17 below. Circle words that are repeated in the passage. What is the significance of these repeated words?

   fruit — obey
   remain — Love each other
   bear fruit — friends
   loved me — Father
   remain in love — choose
   abide in me

   1 I am the true vine, and my Father is the vinedresser.

   2 Every branch in me that does not bear fruit he takes away, and every branch that does bear fruit he prunes, that it may bear more fruit.

   3 Already you are clean because of the word that I have spoken to you.

   4 Abide in me, and I in you. As the branch cannot bear fruit by itself, unless it abides in the vine, neither can you, unless you abide in me.

5 I am the vine; you are the branches. Whoever abides in me and I in him, he it is that bears much fruit, for apart from me you can do nothing.

6 If anyone does not abide in me he is thrown away like a branch and withers; and the branches are gathered, thrown into the fire, and burned.

7 If you abide in me, and my words abide in you, ask whatever you wish, and it will be done for you.

8 By this my Father is glorified, that you bear much fruit and so prove to be my disciples.

9 As the Father has loved me, so have I loved you. Abide in my love.

10 If you keep my commandments, you will abide in my love, just as I have kept my Father's commandments and abide in his love.

11 These things I have spoken to you, that my joy may be in you, and that your joy may be full.

12 This is my commandment, that you love one another as I have loved you.

13 Greater love has no one than this, that someone lay down his life for his friends.

14 You are my friends if you do what I command you.

15 No longer do I call you servants, for the servant does not know what his master is doing; but I have called you friends, for all that I have heard from my Father I have made known to you.

16 *You did not choose me, but I chose you and appointed you that you should go and bear fruit and that your fruit should abide, so that whatever you ask the Father in my name, he may give it to you.*

17 *These things I command you, so that you will love one another.*[21]

2. The passage describes two types of branches: one that remains in the vine and one that does not. Describe in your own words the two types of people these branches represent. Imagine how they might spend their time. What makes them distinct?

> Remain/abide - stay close to God, listens for His word, prays, reads the Word and practices loving/serving.
> Wither - when turn from God's way and don't stay close to the heart of God.

3. Based on the passage, what do you think it means to abide?

   Live in me - stay with me - model me - love me and give love away. (continue w/o fading or being lost)

4. In what specific ways do you hear the Lord asking you to respond? What will you do this week to help you abide more closely with Him?

   Abide - body as a temple - honor

   Abide in loving others, being patient -- seeing wonder walking way of holy

DAY TWO

Today we are going to consider an example of pruning in the life of one of the most important leaders introduced in Genesis. As we read the story of Joseph, I urge you to read it not as a fictional story, but as a definitive history and source of truth. Joseph lived from 1915-1859 B.C. He was the youngest of Jacob's sons. He is 17 years old at the start of this chapter and his mother was Jacob's beloved Rachel. [22] Joseph's story is frequently studied in Christian settings. If you are familiar with the story, consider reading a different translation of the Bible so you can see it with fresh eyes. Let's look together for new insights regarding the planting and pruning God did in Joseph's life.

5. Read Genesis 37. What privileges or gifts does Joseph have? How does he use them?

   Dreams

6. In what ways could what happened to Joseph be an example of pruning? Why might the Lord have allowed this to happen to him?

   To build him up

7. Can you think of a time when God pruned something in your life for His glory and your good? Describe the circumstances and what that felt like.

> Kevin left and made me stronger
> Took job away.
> opened new door

Hebrews 12:6 reminds us that "the Lord disciplines the one he loves, and chastises every son whom he receives."[23] God's love for us runs so deep that He both prunes and disciplines, and ultimately sent His Son to die on a cross for us.

DAY THREE

We will continue the story of Joseph today and read about how the Lord keeps shaping him through pruning. These chapters detail the season when Joseph was enslaved and imprisoned. As you are reading, take note of how his character is maturing and how he is learning to abide with God more deeply.

8. Read Genesis 39 and 40. Where was Joseph transplanted? How does this contrast to the place where Joseph grew up?

    Egypt

9. How does Joseph's relationship with God change in Chapter 39? (Cite a few verses that help you see something new in their relationship.)

    ¹ Lord was with Joseph so he prosp.
    ⁵ Lord blessed household
    ²¹ in prison the Lord was with him
    ²³ and gave him success whatever he did

10. How is God present for Joseph through his season of pruning?

    God never leaves him and is present in protection, blessing, success.

11. What is the special gift Joseph uses in Chapter 40 to help the cup-bearer and baker? What other gifts or qualities are growing in Joseph in this chapter?

   Dreams... interpretations belong to God
   Dream interpreter
   Others depend on him

12. Flip back to Genesis 37 and reread verses 5-11. How has Joseph changed? Who/What made this change possible?

   God made change possible

DAY FOUR

As we finish our study of the life of Joseph, I encourage you to see how this story illuminates who God is and his relationship with Joseph. After waiting *two years* in prison, Joseph has the opportunity to help interpret Pharaoh's dreams. Before you begin reading, think about that time frame. Imagine what Joseph might have experienced in those two years of waiting.

13. Read Genesis 41. How does Joseph describe God in this chapter? What is he revealing to Pharaoh about his God?

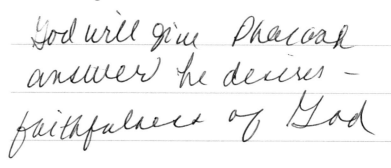
God will give Pharaoh answer he desires – faithfulness of God

14. How does Joseph come to be promoted and what does Pharaoh give him?

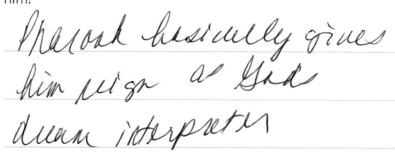
Pharaoh basically gives him reign as God dream interpreter

15. Read Genesis 42. Despite the past, what does this chapter reveal about Joseph's connection to his family? Does he still care for them?

That he loves them

16. We are each created for community. Part of flourishing is helping others flourish. As we saw in our study on Day One this week, abiding and pruning lead to more fruit. How does Joseph have the opportunity to help others flourish in these chapters? Why do you think he conflicted about it?

He is conflicted because of pain brought to him. But he is forgiving — God gives him that

Everything God does is intentional. Nothing is by accident. Every piece is part of His plan. Joseph's story is a reminder of this. Joseph's story also points to Jesus' story and how his death was part of God's plan to reconcile us to Him.

DAY FIVE

We are going to skip ahead in this story and read some specific passages for the questions below. If you are not as familiar with the story, I encourage you to read chapters 43-47 in their entirety. You won't want to miss a thing.

17. Read Chapter 45:1-15. What does this encounter with his brothers reveal about the pruning process for Joseph? What fruit is evident in him now?

    Fruit of forgiveness and faithfulness/obedience to God

18. Read Chapter 45:16-28. Joseph served Pharaoh and his people. What is Pharaoh's response when he hears Joseph's family has come? How is Joseph's service to Pharaoh extended to Joseph's family?

    Pharaoh extends grace to all his family

19. Joseph and Jacob are finally reunited in Chapter 46. Read verses 28-30. Why is this meeting so powerful? What does it display about both Joseph and Jacob?

    Jacob lets go and lets God for the powerful reunion

20. Joseph's family is then transplanted to the land of Egypt. This land was, at one time, the place of Joseph's enslavement and imprisonment, but now is his home. Read Genesis 47. How does the Lord allow Joseph to leverage his privileges to help his family and all of Egypt flourish?

He allows his family to live well

Though we can't see how God is using each event in our lives to orchestrate His sovereign plan, we do know the He is good in all things. Romans 8:32 reminds us, "He who did not spare his own Son, but gave him up for us all—how will he not also, along with him, graciously give us all things?"[24]

[Margin note: This is my sea change.]

DAY SIX

Shauna Niequist, author of *Present Over Perfect*, writes, "But here's the thing: every new season of life is an invitation to leave behind the things of the season before, the trappings and traps that have long expired, right for then, no longer right for now. Whatever passage you're facing ... has the potential to be your sea-change, your invitation to leave behind what's not essential and travel deeply into the heart of things."[25] Take a few minutes to reflect on these words and how they relate to pruning.

21. Make a list of all your present commitments. (Think about all the little and big things that require your time.)

    Food / need simplicity Financial Exercise
    Work balance / need better alignment
    Finish coaching

22. Do any of these commitments feel heavy? Are any of these commitments capturing too much of your time or ruling your identity? Has anything become an idol to you? Pray over these lists. Hold them up to the light of Truth and surrender to His plan for you.

    Is work idol —
    how do I continue my calling
    Idol helping Kevin

23. James 1:5 reminds us, "If any of you lacks wisdom, you should ask God, who gives generously to all without finding fault, and it will be given to you." Write a prayer asking God to show you any commitments you might need to say goodbye to in this next season. Ask him to strengthen you in the areas and commitments you feel led to keep.

Lord show me the way. Show me what should fall by wayside and what should stay.

Let this be my sea change. Use me mold me for a greater good.

Abundance

WEEK THREE
REST

One of my favorite places to go on a late summer night is Moravia Winery—just a short drive from our home in Fresno, California. Somehow even when it's scorching outside, it's a few degrees cooler at the winery. My kids love to play wild and free with their friends on the pirate ship play structure. Some of the daddies play bocce ball. We lounge on picnic blankets and share goodies. They often have a live band playing music and a food truck selling burritos or a vendor serving up fancy cupcakes. As the sun lies down for the evening, ribbons of color dance beyond the rows and rows of vines dripping with grapes.

Shawn and I got engaged in August. I was dreaming of a wedding at Moravia, but we had to consider the seasons. Our wedding was slated for January. If you drive out to the winery during the winter months, you will witness a different scene from the flourishing vines of late summer/early fall. Mysterious fog often seeps in late at night and early in the mornings. The vines are pruned back, standing stark against the winter sky. They have traded green leaves and lush grapes for gnarly and naked vines. This season in the vine's life is called dormancy, the resting period before new growth.

Rest is necessary not just in the cycle of the grape's life, but also in our human lives. Our hearts are restless until they find rest in God. Rest refreshes the mind, body and spirit. And yet, our American culture lies to us about rest. We are led to believe that time is money; those who multi-task best are the most productive; and there is no time for rest. The Bible tells us just the opposite. In Matthew 11:28-30, Jesus leans in and shares these words with the crowd: "Come to me, all of you who are weary and carry heavy burdens, and I will give you rest. Take my yoke upon you. Let me teach you, because I am humble and gentle at heart, and you will find rest for your souls. For my yoke is easy to bear, and the burden I give you is light."[17] Jesus speaks of a different kind of yoke. Margaret Feinberg helps unpack this passage: "With this invitation, Jesus instructs disciples not to take on the yoke of the religious leaders that were heavy and burdensome but to take on his yoke, his teaching—one that's marked by love, forgiveness, grace, and rest."[18] Jesus' deep desire revealed in this passage is for His people to experience a deep soul rest.

The idea of rest originates in Genesis. It was part of God's plan from the very beginning. God worked for six days creating the world. The creation narrative reveals a definite rhythm. God spoke the light, sky, earth, sea, plants, sun, moon and living creatures into being. Then He leaned in closer to create Adam and Eve in His image. He breathed life into them. In Genesis 2, there is a divine pause, an emphasis on rest, a mark of completion: "So the heavens and the earth and everything in them were completed. By the seventh day God completed His work that he had done, and He rested on the seventh day from all His work that he had done. God blessed the seventh day and declared it holy, for on it He rested from His work of creation."[19] Why would the God of the universe, who has an endless supply of energy and power, take time to rest? Why would the idea of resting after work be repeated and emphasized? He wanted to model this rhythm of work and rest. That day of rest was called the "Sabbath" in Hebrew. The day of rest is blessed and holy as the passage highlights.

The importance of rest is reiterated in a different way in the Psalms. In Psalm 3, the Hebrew word "selah" appears for the first time. "Selah" is repeated three times at the end of verse 2 and 4, and serves as the final word of the Psalm. Although the exact definition of this word is unknown, scholars believe it was likely a musical or liturgical term that referred to silence, pause or interlude. "Selah" occurs 71 times in the Psalms.[20] Speaking in musical terms, the rests between the notes are just as important as the notes themselves. These create the rhythm of a song. David understood this and displayed it in the writing of the Psalms, which were used to lead worship. Selah points back to the Sabbath or day of rest established in the Creation narrative.

Jesus models rest throughout his life and ministry. On several occasions, he takes time to pause, rest and pray. We see an example of this in Mark 6:31-32: "Then Jesus said, 'Let's go off by ourselves to a quiet place and rest awhile.' He said this because there were so many people coming and going that Jesus and his apostles didn't even have time to eat. So they left by boat for a quiet place, where they could be alone."[21] Jesus is leading the disciples into a place of rest. He sees how the ministry and crowds are draining to them, and he gives them permission to take some time away.

Taking time to rest is counterintuitive for most Americans. Our cities do not sleep. Other cultures have a natural rhythm of rest. I remember when I lived in Central America, the people took "siestas" or naps in the afternoons. Some stores even closed down for the napping hour. My friend, who lives in Germany, tells me businesses close down for the entire weekend to allow for family and rest time. This would be hard to fathom in our American context.

I grew up in a house where we were constantly busy and involved. In elementary school, my evenings were filled with piano lessons, soccer games, ballet and jazz classes, church youth group and more. In junior high and high school, I added activities like newspaper, yearbook, Track & Field, and voice lessons. While I enjoyed all these activities, I remember we were always running, always pushing deadlines, always melting into bed at night exhausted. I am grateful for the many amazing opportunities my parents gave me, but sometimes I wonder if it also was training me to chase busyness.

Growing up and leaving my parents' house, I continued on this trajectory— filling my schedule with a myriad of fun activities and too often shunning rest for service projects and social gatherings. The Bible warns in Psalm

127:2 against this kind of pace: "It is in vain that you rise up early and go late to rest, eating the bread of anxious toil; for he gives to his beloved sleep."[22] We were not created to burn the candle at both ends. We need to stop the striving and trade performance for rest in Him. Rebekah Lyons speaks to this in her book, *You Are Free*: "I'd always thought my closeness with Jesus was dependent on me. Consequently, I was an Energizer bunny for him. But Jesus' love draws us in for one thing: to come into his presence and his rest, to stop working and doing and striving, to remain in him. That's it."[23] Lyons highlights that it's our presence, not our performance Jesus cares about.

Rest is the way we detox from the busyness. Rest may look different for different people, depending on how they are wired. If we have gone through a season of pruning, it may take some time to recalibrate and make rest a part of our new rhythm. I found this to be true last summer after I pruned some big branches from my life. At first, I didn't know how to rest. I felt anxious and uncomfortable with the extra time in my schedule. I felt guilty for taking time for myself instead of working, serving or being with my family.

Then I learned a new rhythm of rest in an unexpected way. I signed up to run a marathon. I know what you're thinking: running 26.2 miles is not resting. That's mostly true. I put together a training schedule with the help of my hubby-coach, who is also an endurance athlete. My schedule included four days a week of running and two days of strength training. As I ran, I talked to God. I discovered the runs afforded me the time and space to grieve the past and the things I had pruned from my life. The miles were hard but they became a precious time of connecting with my Father. They were like a scheduled Daddy date.

I had one problem. I was training in the summer months in Fresno, California. The average daytime temperatures were in the triple digits. I don't do well exercising when it's that hot. I quickly discovered if I wanted to beat the heat, I had to wake up early! Let's just be clear: I am a night owl by nature. In different seasons, I have trained myself to wake up early, but I always feel like a night owl masquerading as an early bird. It's not pretty.

The irony in this is that running taught me to rest. That combination of waking up early and running long miles left me naturally exhausted by the afternoon. I had to build naptime into my day or I would be a crabby mess by dinner time. (For those of you who have toddlers, you know exactly what I'm talking about). My husband encouraged me that the rest was just as important as the runs because my body needed to recover. He explained that when we do a hard workout we are breaking down muscle. When we rest, the body has time to rebuild on a cellular level and the muscles are built up even stronger than before.

I started a resting hour with my kids (ages 4, 7 and 10 at the time). They were allowed to read books, color or sleep. The house was quiet. Mommy had permission to nap. When my husband got home from work, he would ask me about my day. He congratulated me when I told him I had napped. The first time he praised me for resting, I was shocked. I don't ever remember my mom napping when I was a kid. When my girls were younger, rest was often sabotaged by one of them needing something. I often gave up. He was helping me retrain my brain and body to embrace the benefits of rest.

Psalm 46 speaks of looking to God as our refuge and strength, of not being moved and trusting God to help us. One of my favorite verses is Psalm 46:10: "Be still and know that I am God."[24] Those words have also challenged my attitude about rest. The command is to actually be still with our bodies and our minds. My husband coached me that even just laying down and not moving can be a resting state. At first when I tried to nap,

> **Seeds of Truth:**
>
> *"If we want to live a wholehearted life, we have to become intentional about cultivating rest and play, and we must work to let go of exhaustion as a status symbol and productivity as self-worth.*
>
> —Brene Brown

my mind would race all over the place. I would craft to-do lists in my head. I would worry about things. I had to return to the words of Psalm 46:10 and get in the habit of *being still*—both body and mind.

Margaret Feinberg writes, "In resisting busyness, we can once again restake our claim as wholly loved by God and flourish in the joy of being his children. This frees us from the bondage of overproduction and liberates us; our hearts lie fallow to receive God's goodness and grace."[25] God is calling each one of us into sweet Sabbath rest. This might look different for you than it does for me. You will need to work it out in your attitude, your schedule and your family context. However, I do know that it involves turning down the noise around us and entering into His presence. I invite you to a place of rest this week so you can abide in the Vine. Rest is a gift from a Good Father who longs to see us flourish.

FLOURISHING TOGETHER

DAY ONE

Read Jesus' words in Matthew 11:28-30 in The Message version below.

> "Are you tired? Worn out? Burned out on religion? Come to me. Get away with me and you'll recover your life. I'll show you how to take a real rest.
>
> Walk with me and work with me—watch how I do it. Learn the unforced rhythms of grace. I won't lay anything heavy or ill-fitting on you.
>
> Keep company with me and you'll learn to live freely and lightly."[27]

> **Meditate & Memorize:**
>
> "Come to me, all of you who are weary and carry heavy burdens, and I will give you rest."
>
> —Matthew 11:28[26]

1. Are there any words or phrases in this version that speak to you? Is there something in these verses you needed to hear from the Lord today?

   Finding unforced rhythms of grace — rest, recover.

2. What do you think the "unforced rhythms of grace" are referring to in this passage? Describe what this could look like in your life.

   Be in nature
   Find mysteries of rhythm
   Rest — restore

3. Do you feel weary? Are you burdened? What kind of yoke do you carry? Write a prayer about the areas where you feel weary and tired. Ask God to help you plan for times of rest even if your schedule feels busy. Obediently respond when He shows you the ways He would have you rest.

When I feel weary Lord, restore me. Give me strength for the joy of the work and rest to be restored.

Because of Christ's death and resurrection, those who belong to Him are hidden in Him. It is His life being lived out in us as it says in Galatians 2:20. Surrender all to Him, trusting Him to be enough.

DAY TWO

Today we are going to look at a picture of what it looks like to rest at Jesus' feet. There are several Marys in the Bible who were friends of Jesus and integral to his ministry. We know Jesus' mother was Mary. There was also Mary Magdalene and Mary of Bethany. This week we will be learning about Mary of Bethany. Some of you may know her as Martha and Lazarus' sister. Mary was not just a sister. She was a woman who sat at Jesus feet whenever he was around. She positioned herself in His presence and was hungry to learn from him. She recognized him to be not just a gifted rabbi but the Messiah.[28]

4. Jesus is traveling and goes to visit Mary and Martha. Read Luke 10:38-42. Describe his interaction with Martha.

   Martha wants Jesus to take notice that Mary is not helping in prep – Jesus says she chose the better

5. Write down a few details about the way Mary interacts with Jesus.

   sat at Lord's feet listening to Jesus

6. How is Mary taking a posture of rest in this scene? How does Jesus commend her for this choice?

   She is listening, absorbing, taking in and resting in Jesus.
   She chose better.

7. How does this help us define rest? Is this rest active or passive?

   It should passive (yet active) listening —

8. What takeaway is there for you in this story? What does this passage speak to you personally about rest and flourishing?

   I need rest — but it should be nourishing and I can rest in Christ.

DAY THREE

Today we are going to explore a different section of scripture that features Mary and Martha. Yesterday we witnessed their interaction with Jesus. From this passage, is clear they have a close relationship with Jesus. Read John 11:1-44. In this passage, we will see how Jesus cares deeply for His friends and carves out time to grieve with them.

9. What does John 11:1-5 show us about Jesus and his relationship with Mary, Martha and Lazarus?

    He cared and loved them all

10. Why do you think Jesus stayed two days longer before he traveled to Bethany to see his friends? Does this trouble you?

    What Jesus did had purpose — so there was a reason — even though not revealed.

11. Describe Mary's actions when Jesus comes to Bethany. How do you imagine she feels?

    She runs to him wishing he was there earlier.

12. Jesus is deeply moved and takes time to weep with Mary. Why is this significant to the story?

Because even then he is showing suffering and grief

13. Have you ever felt Jesus was with you during a time of grief? Describe that situation.

Yes - through signs ii Ryan monarch butterfly, through cardinal ii doll. And each time a peace that passes understanding

Jesus' delay was motivated by His love! He knew that it would glorify the Son, and therefore be for their (and our) good. God's love for us is most clearly evidenced by the way He gave His Son so we could believe, as it says in John 3:16.

DAY FOUR

Moving from the death of Lazarus and Jesus' tender compassion, today we are going to explore another famous scene, which involves Mary of Bethany. Read John 12:1-8 and witness the way one woman showed her deep love for Jesus.

14. What is Mary's status or position?

    Mary is a servant

15. How does she jeopardize or leverage her position in these verses?

    Jeopardizes in others' eyes but not in Jesus' — he rebukes and affirms

16. Mary expresses her love for Jesus in a radical way. What were some of the responses of the people who observed this act?

    Others did not understand but she courageously showed her love

17. How does Jesus respond to those who question Mary's expression of love?

   With welcome and has others leave her alone

18. How have you seen Mary flourish through these three accounts of her interaction with Jesus?

   Yes she listened deeply, followed and showed radical love

19. In what ways has your heart seen Jesus differently? How have you been changed by what you have seen?

   I am changed by the cross. The act sacrifice and great love — how does it change me?

DAY FIVE

In her book, *Nothing to Prove*, Jennie Allen, talks about the importance of the right kind of rest. She says, "When Jesus promises us rest, He almost always is talking about *soul rest*. It's why most of the ways we try to rest actually make our insides more chaotic. TV, sleep, Facebook surfing—all fall short because nothing but Jesus can bring rest to the chaos inside us.... Our confidence comes from believing God can do anything, then stepping back and letting Him."[29]

20. How do you respond to this idea? What are some ways you "rest" or take a break that are not healthy for healing the inner chaos? Write out your responses in a journal entry or prayer in the space below.

21. Read through a Psalm and write out a verse or section of the Psalm that speaks to your heart, giving you rest for your soul.

DAY SIX

22. Take some time today to rest. Give yourself permission to lay down and listen to worship music or take a nap. Quiet your body, and pray for God to help you quiet your mind and soul during this time. At the end of the day, consider reflecting on what the Lord spoke to you in that time.

_____

_____

_____

_____

_____

_____

_____

_____

_____

_____

In Genesis, we learn about God's original purpose of the Sabbath. Jesus reiterates God's intent in Mark 2:27 when he says "The Sabbath was made for man, not man for the Sabbath."

WEEK FOUR
NOURISH

*All winter
she waited
wondered
rested
until one day
in the deep soil
of anticipation and
grief
she felt the ground
around her
warming
She felt her strength
rising
pushing
through the transition
the pain was acute
there, but the
shadow was lifted
And now
fully rooted
well-nourished
she extended her
arms in abandon
upwards toward the
Light
She burst through the
hardened earth -
a flash of fire -
her petals singing
Spring.*

After my run the other day, I stopped in my tracks at the sight of this fiery-red-orange freesia blooming in front of my house. She inspired poetry. After weeks of winter rains and colder temperatures, this bold flower seemed to say, "Behold, spring is here!"

I did not plant her there. She was a gift that came with our house when we bought it. I first noticed her bloom last spring. She is a perennial, meaning she is a plant that produces new growth every year. The word perennial

NOURISH

literally means "present at all seasons of the year, persisting, regularly repeated or renewed."[30] The freesia reminds me of the familiar words of Ecclesiastes 1:1: "There is a time for everything, and a season for every activity under the heavens."[31] There are seasons to rest, seasons to nourish, and seasons to bloom. She speaks to me of the "unforced rhythms of grace"[32] as it talks about in Matthew 11:29 that endure and help us to continually be renewed.

I learned in second grade that a plant needs three major things to grow: water, soil and light. If plants are not regularly nourished in this way, they wither, wilt or their growth may be stunted altogether. In the same way, we humans need certain things to nourish our bodies and souls so we can be whole and grow. At the basic level, we need a balance of water, food, exercise, and sleep. At the soul level, we need deep connection with God and relationships with others.

After my husband died in 2014, I realized I desperately needed to take some time to nourish myself and my three daughters again. From the day he had received the initial stage four cancer diagnosis to the day he graduated to Heaven, we had lived in crisis mode. During those months, I slept very little. I cared for my husband around the clock as the cancer coursed through his body. He needed medicine and special foods every hour. I traveled with him to many doctor appointments and even stayed with him in the hospital for three days. In his final weeks, he needed help with basic hygiene and trips to the bathroom. When friends or family members came to relieve me in taking care of him, I could never actually rest because I was so fraught with anxiety. I experienced anticipatory grief. I couldn't keep down much of my own food, and it showed in the amount of weight I lost that summer. I was withering.

After the funeral, the meals began to arrive. My people began to nourish us with food. They delivered enchilada casserole, sausage lasagna, curried butternut squash soup and pan-roasted salmon. They served up salads and crusty bread. They baked us decadent chocolate cake and buttery cookies. People took us out to our favorite restaurants and even sent us gift cards for our favorite local grocery stores. I realized then how malnourished I was. All my resources had been depleted by being a caretaker. I needed to eat literally, but more than that, I needed the nourishment of my community. I needed people to sit with us at the table over and over again until it didn't feel so empty without him. I needed courage to step into a new normal and make new memories with my daughters.

In 1 Corinthians 6:19-20, the Apostle Paul challenges the church of Corinth with these words: "Or didn't you realize that your body is a sacred place, the place of the Holy Spirit? Don't you see that you can't live however you please, squandering what God paid such a high price for? The physical part of you is not some piece of property belonging to the spiritual part of you. God owns the whole works. So let people see God in and through your body."[33] Those words challenge me too. I have a responsibility to take care of my body not because the world tells me self-care is an important value, but because the Bible tells me my body is a sacred place of the Holy Spirit. Both the physical and spiritual parts of us need nourishment.

On a practical level, we can nourish ourselves through life-giving activities that connect us with God. For me, that means carving out time to go for a hike in the mountains, or creating a new recipe, or reading a book on the beach, or even spending quality time over coffee with a heart-friend. I need to be careful to choose activities that reconnect me with the Father, that restore me and help me to flourish. I like to call it "soul care." Sometimes it's easier to numb out on social media, television or even use self-care time to catch up on errands or laundry, but those things do not really refresh and restore me.

Jesus promised bread from heaven in John 6. "I am the bread of life," Jesus told the disciples. "No one who comes to Me will ever be hungry and no one who believes in Me will ever be thirsty again."[34] Jesus drew the connection in these verses that He is the bread of eternal life. We all can choose to be nourished by believing in Him and partaking in the spiritual food He provides. For believers today, we can draw nourishment by reading God's Word and applying it to our daily lives. This is key to flourishing.

Jesus also promised us a living water that will always quench our thirst. In John 4, Jesus entered into conversation with a Samaritan woman at the well. Jesus said to her, "Everyone who drinks from this water will get thirsty again. But whoever drinks from the water that I will give him will never get thirsty again—ever! In fact, the water I will give him will become a well of water springing up within him for eternal life."[35] Jesus knew this woman had a parched soul. She thirsted for something more meaningful—something men were not able to provide in her life. She needed a well that did not run dry. She needed to be with Jesus.

In her book, *Nothing to Prove*, Jennie Allen writes about this: "Being with Jesus, who is the vine, moves water and nourishment into and through us as branches. Connection to Him is how our thirsty souls are quenched and also how we receive a steady supply of the water required to produce mature, sweet-tasting fruit."[36] The Samaritan woman spent time talking with Jesus at the well and her life was forever changed. She then ran and poured out to others. When we spend time talking with Jesus in prayer, we, too, will be changed. Our thirst for a more abundant life can be quenched in that space of relationship.

Jesus' words are also powerful because they foreshadow three chapters later in John 7: 37 when Jesus talks about the "streams of living water."[37] Although this is a familiar metaphor used throughout the Old Testament, this time Jesus told the desert-dwelling crowd about the "living water" to point to the gift of the Holy Spirit. The Helper will be poured out on the disciples after Jesus' death and resurrection. We as believers have access to the Holy Spirit, who flows through us today. When we feel thirsty, we can pray for the Holy Spirit to intervene and guide us. And then the living water can flow through us onto others.

Finally, we need light to grow. Did you ever do one of those science projects in elementary school where you planted a seed and watched it grow over time? Last year my daughter's class planted bean seeds in soil in little Styrofoam cups. They set them in the window sill at the front of the school so the seeds could get sunlight. Those seeds softened and broke open. The light filtered through the window and awakened growth. Little green stems appeared and pushed their way upward out of the soil, eventually developing into bean plants.

In the same way, the light of our Heavenly Father helps nourish us to push through the hard soil of our lives and grow. In 2 Corinthians 4:6, the prophet Isaiah shares this message: "For God, who said, 'Let light shine out of darkness,' made his light shine in our hearts to give us the light of the knowledge of God's glory displayed in the face of Christ."[38] God brings light into our dark souls and the dark circumstances of our lives. He reveals Himself to us through the Holy Spirit and His word. He invites us to be nourished in Him and experience His glory.

QUICK REFERENCE: EVENTS IN THE BOOK OF ESTHER

- 483 B.C.—Queen Vashti deposed from her position (Esther 1:19)
- 478 B.C.—King Xerxes calls for all the beautiful, young women from across the kingdom to be brought into his harem so he can choose a new queen (Esther 2:3)
- 478 B.C.—Mordecai, Esther's cousin and father figure, thwarts a conspiracy (Esther 2:21)
- 474 B.C.—Haman, the king's advisor, seeks revenge on the Jews (Esther 3:6)
- 474 B.C. Mordecai shares with Esther about Haman's plot to annihilate the Jews (Esther 4:6-9)
- 473 B.C.—Esther urges Mordecai to gather all of the Jews to fast and pray for three days on her behalf (Esther 3:16)
- 473 B.C.—Esther prepares a banquet for the king and Haman (Esther 5:4)
- 473 B.C.—Esther reveals Haman's plan to the king (Esther 7:3-6)
- 473 B.C.—Haman is hanged on the gallows he built (Esther 7:9)
- 473 B.C.—King Xerxes issues and edict on behalf of Esther and the Jews (Esther 8:11)
- 472. B.C.—The Purim celebration is instituted to commemorate freedom for the Jews (Esther 9:17-18)
- 472 B.C.—King Xerxes offers a tribute to Mordecai (Esther 10:3)

(Source: Bible Hub, "Esther timeline," Accessed December 3, 2017, http://biblehub.com/timeline/esther/1.htm.)

Seeds of Truth:

"In resisting busyness, we once again restake our claim as wholly loved by God and flourish in the joy of being his children. This frees us from the bondage of overproduction and liberates us; our hearts lie fallow to receive God's goodness and grace."

—Margaret Feinberg, *Flourish* (154-155)

DAY ONE

This week we are going to delve into the book of Esther. This is the story of a Jewish, orphan-girl-turned-queen. Esther grows up as a minority in her culture because she is a Jew. She is raised by her cousin, Mordecai, with very little, but she is called to the palace into a place of great privilege. God uses this faithful woman in a powerful way. If this is a book you are familiar with, I challenge you to read this story in a new version of the Bible. Press in to notice some new details that you might not have noticed before.

1. Read Esther Chapter 1. Make a list of some of the details that stood out as important in this chapter.

2. Read Esther Chapter 2. How would you describe the relationship between Esther and her cousin Mordecai?

Meditate & Memorize:

"As the rain and the snow come down from heaven, and do not return to it without watering the earth and making it bud and flourish, so that it yields seed for the sower and bread for the eater, so is my word that goes out from my mouth: It will not return to me empty, but will accomplish what I desire and achieve the purpose for which I sent it."

—Isaiah 55:10-11[39]

3. There were certain cultural practices during this time period to help prepare the women to meet the king. What are some of these practices described in Esther 2:12?

DAY TWO

Today we are going to continue reading the book of Esther, paying attention to the values that are important to each person in the story. Continue reading the story of Esther in Chapter 3.

4. How would you describe Haman's character? What is most important to him?

5. Read Esther Chapter 4. Take special note of Esther's response in Esther 4:15-17. What does she do before she steps up to confront the king? How do you think this prepared her?

6. Esther has a unique ability to gather community in this scene. Why is community important to her nourishment?

DAY THREE

Today we are going to witness the way Esther has chosen to feed her soul affects the outcome of her circumstances. Continue reading the story of Esther in Chapter 5.

7. How does Esther prepare herself for meeting the king with her request?

8. What is the king's response? How does he receive her?

9. Skip ahead to read Esther Chapter 7. Pay particular attention to Esther 7:3-4. How does Esther form her request to the king?

10. What did Haman seek to feed his ego versus what Esther sought to nourish her soul? What was the result of both of their seeking?

We have seen God's faithfulness to His people, as well as His sense of justice in these chapters. Both faithfulness and justice are evidenced later in Jesus, who satisfied God's need for justice when He died in our place.

DAY FOUR

Today we are going to continue reading Esther, Chapter 8.

11. In Esther 8:8, the king grants Esther and Mordecai an important privilege. How would you describe that privilege and why is it such a huge turn of events?

12. What does this show about God's sovereignty?

13. How does this encourage you in your faith?

14. Where is God asking you to courageously obey Him today? How will you respond?

DAY FIVE

In her book, *The Broken Way*, Ann Voskamp refers to the story of Esther. She calls out an "Esther Generation" as women who will "defy cynical indifference by making a critical difference."[40] She champions Esther for the way she gathers her people and fights on behalf of the most vulnerable. Esther was devoted to God, and therefore, risked herself for His people.

 writes, "We belong to each other because we all mutually indwell each other, and there is nothing worth having inside the gate when we've got pieces of ourselves outside the gate...That's why the Esther Generation risks everything for those outside the gate—because they hold the necessary pieces of our collective soul, which we need for shalom. Wholeness."[41] Although Esther lived "inside the gate" or in the palace with certain privileges, she had a heart of compassion for those "outside the gate," who were vulnerable and needed to be rescued.

15. Who are the most vulnerable in your community? Who stands outside the gate?

    _____

    _____

    _____

16. How might you leverage your privileges like Esther did for those who stand outside the gate?

    _____

    _____

    _____

17. 17. God served as our example of sacrificing on behalf of others. In John 3:16, we are reminded that God so loved us that He gave up His only Son on our behalf. How does risking for another's freedom help all of us flourish?

DAY SIX

18. How do you engage in soul care? If you do not have regular spiritual nourishment in your life right now, make a plan to change that. Jot some ideas below. Pray over them. Invite someone to hold you accountable to nourish yourself regularly.

18. Have you ever had an experience where you felt rested after you engaged in soul care? Describe what you did and how you felt.

WEEK FIVE
CULTIVATE

I grew up in Chicago in a neighborhood where the houses were like little boxes made of brick all sitting in neat rows along the street. We had a small backyard—not big enough for playing kickball or a trampoline—just a little plot of green grass with a grill and space for a few garden boxes. My mama wasn't too worried about the size of our garden. She just loved to make things grow. Every spring we would help her pick out seeds and plants from our local nursery. She would give my brother and me little shovels and spading forks. Our assignment was to break up the hard soil to get it ready for planting.

Mom would buy a big bag of top soil with organic fertilizer and we would mix it in with the rest of the hard, broken up soil. The dark, soft top soil would mix with the gray, ashy soil that had endured Chicago's winter in the garden boxes. Mom helped us dig out little holes to slip our seeds into. We covered the holes with more nutrient-rich soil and patted the tops firmly. We used the hose or a watering can to wet the mounds of soil.

Then came the waiting.

While we waited, we dreamed of making homemade Italian pesto and marinara sauce with our herbs and tomatoes. We salivated over wax beans and red peppers we could add to our salads. We made lists of favorites like Mom's moist zucchini bread or eggplant parmigiana we could create with our prized garden vegetables. We longed for the fruit of our garden to emerge.

Finally, after several days and sometimes weeks, we watched as little heads of green sprouted from the soil and stretched upward toward the sun. The growth was always slow at first but surprised me later in the summer when we would have towering tomato plants or zucchini chasing across the planter boxes in abundance.

Somehow I've never gotten a garden to flourish quite the way my mama did. I didn't inherit her green thumb, but she taught me a lot about the process of gardening. Mostly it's about putting in the work, being patient, and getting to know your plants. The word "cultivate" means to prepare and foster growth in order to raise crops. We had to cultivate the garden in our urban Chicago backyard to help it grow. We had to work the soil, water and tend to the plants.

Outside of the garden box, cultivate means to develop or improve by education, to train, and to encourage.[42] Growth requires hard work and sacrifice. It doesn't just happen overnight. The season of growth is different from pruning, resting and nourishing. To cultivate requires tilling the soil, sorting through our priorities and carving out time for learning. The growth season also requires moving through transition into the development of our faith and our character. Sometimes this means pushing through the hard earth of suffering, disappointment, fear, rejection, and even loneliness. It may mean learning tough lessons from our mistakes or devoting extra energy and time to follow a dream.

I recently had the opportunity to hear pastor and author Mark Batterson speak at a conference. He said something that made me pause: "In God's economy, things happen at the speed of a seed."[43] Batterson's point was that growth takes time. We can't just speed it along. We can't dictate the pace or measure the amount of work it will require ahead of time. We do know that if we allow the Master Gardener to do His work in us, He is always working toward flourishing. Isaiah 61:11 says, "For as the soil makes the sprout come up and a garden causes seeds to grow, so the Sovereign LORD will make righteousness and praise spring up before all nations."[44] God is in the business of cultivating and growing His Kingdom, and we are invited to participate in that work.

This week we will be studying the story of Rahab. She is what you might call an unexpected heroine. She wasn't perfect. She wasn't a leader with a big platform. She was in many ways positioned in the right place at the right time. In fact, Rahab had a sordid past but God still used her to grow His garden in a significant way. She had a tiny mustard seed of faith.[45] She believed the God of Israel was powerful, and she acted on that faith to protect His people. Her courageous act of obedience changed the trajectory of her life and landed her a prime spot in the genealogy of Jesus Christ. She was granted a privilege, which she leveraged for others in the garden. As a result, she and her family were saved. Rahab's story is a reminder that God can use anyone to grow and multiply His Kingdom.

We are often quick to discredit ourselves or look to others who appear to have more vibrant talents, gifts or leadership skills than we do. But all of us are needed in the garden. God has a special purpose for each and every one of us. He created each of us to grow in different ways. I remember one year I started a garden in my home in Fresno, California. That summer, my husband and I were traveling a lot so we enlisted my dad to help us with watering. We had tomatoes, cucumbers, eggplant, zucchini and some other vegetables planted in our garden. After a few weeks of being gone, I came home to some tomato and cucumber plants that were so big they were climbing over the edge of the garden boxes. I was so excited about taking in the harvest and getting creative in the kitchen.

Right away I rushed out to gather the ripe vegetables. The cucumbers were ginormous. We had cucumber salads in all different varieties. The green onions and eggplants were also abundant. I was dreaming about fried eggplant and baba ganoush dip for days. However, the tomatoes were tiny, and there were very few. I was puzzled at first but kept gathering cucumbers. Finally, after a few more days, I called my mom and asked if she had any idea what was happening to our tomatoes. The plants were huge but there was no fruit.

> **Seeds of Truth:**
>
> *"Fruit grows in seasons, and all seasons are necessary for growing it. And seasons are as much about what is not happening as what is. It has as much to do with inactivity as with activity, waiting as with working, barrenness as with abundance, dormancy as with vitality."*
>
> —Mark Batterson, *Spiritual Rhythm: Being with Jesus Every Season of Your Soul*, Introduction

She came over later that day and solved the mystery for us. The tomatoes were being overwatered. My dad loves to water the garden. In the blazing summer sun, he thought the more water, the better crop. He watered all of our plants every day in our absence. Sometimes multiple times a day. He was really getting the job done. Unfortunately, too much water is too much of a good thing when it comes to tomatoes. The cucumbers, for example, were slurping the water right up, but the tomatoes couldn't handle it.

Perhaps the secret of gardening is really getting to know our plants. It's about knowing what kind of plant we are, what kind of soil we thrive in, what amount of water and nutrients we need, and pursuing the things that help us grow. Part of our job is to pursue our God-designed purpose. Author Annie Downs says it this way in her book, *Let's All Be Brave*, "You know what your call to courage is. As we grow in knowledge and understanding of how God made us, we also get to grow in our understanding of the talents he's put in our hands."[46]

This week, I'm inviting you to explore the garden of your soul. What do you need to cultivate in this season? Where can you carve out time and space to grow? How can you soak in the nutrients God has provided and share them with others? We are each called to flourish in the garden. We can encourage others to step into the rich soil cultivated by the Master Gardener to flourish as well. Let's dig in together.

DAY ONE

In Matthew 13, Jesus shares several parables or stories with agricultural and flourishing themes. In the first week of this study, we looked at "The Parable of the Sower." Let's look at another famous parable Jesus shared, "The Parable of the Mustard Seed." Read Matthew 13:31-32.

1. What do you know about mustard seeds? Do a little research and jot down some notes about the size, shape and uniqueness of mustard seeds.

2. What does the mustard seed become? Return to the verses and note how the tree is described?

3. The text says this parable is talking about the Kingdom of God and the birds likely referred to Gentile believers.[46] What do you learn about His Kingdom and its growth through this parable?

> **Meditate & Memorize:**
>
> *"The kingdom of heaven is like a mustard seed that a man took and sowed in his field. It's the smallest of all the seeds, but when grown, it's taller than the vegetables and becomes a tree, so that the birds of the sky come and nest in its branches."*
>
> —Matthew 13:31-32[47]

4. How has His Kingdom grown in your heart?

The Kingdom is here now as it says in Matthew 3:2. By acknowledging our sin before a holy God and accepting the gift of salvation because of Jesus' death on the cross, we are invited to enter that Kingdom.

DAY TWO

Tomorrow we will be looking at the story of Rahab and the important role she took on in the history of Jesus' bloodline. Let's begin by delving into some context for Rahab's story. The book of Joshua was written initially to the nation of Israel, reaching out to the new generation who were entering the promised land. The promised land was in a strategic location, bridging Asia and Africa.[49] Read Joshua Chapter 1.

5. How does God equip Joshua in verses 1-10?

6. What does the Lord specifically command Joshua to do?

7. How does this prepare or cultivate Joshua for what is to come?

8. How does Joshua then ready the people for what lies ahead in verse 10-18?

9. The word "courageous" is repeated several times in this chapter. Why is this word significant to the idea of cultivating?

10. Write out a verse from this chapter that serves as an encouragement to you.

DAY THREE

Rahab was a Canaanite woman living in Jericho. She was an innkeeper and a prostitute. Her house was likely built over the gap between the two walls surrounding the city.[50] These details give us a window to what shaped her identity prior to meeting the Israelite men. Read Joshua Chapter 2.

11. Why are the Israelite men sent to Jericho?

12. How does Rahab protect these men?

13. What did Rahab know about the God of Israel?

Seeds of Truth:

"Fruit means that when people taste your life, you taste like Jesus. If you are fully grafted into Jesus, the vine, then He says your life should produce tangible results that make people say, 'Now that is Christlike.'"

—Banning Liebscher, *Rooted* (p. 2)

14. What did she boldly ask for from the men? What do they promise her?

15. What do you think is the symbolism behind the scarlet cord?

Scarlet is the color of Jesus blood by which we are saved. According to Isaiah 53:5, "by his wounds we are healed."[51]

FLOURISHING TOGETHER

DAY FOUR

Rahab's quick thinking, creativity and courageous response saved her life and the life of her family. Her reverence and obedience to God also wins her a spot in the Genealogy of Jesus. Read Matthew 1:5-6.

16. Who did Rahab eventually marry? Who was her son?

17. Why is this significant?

18. Hebrews 11 is known as the "Hall of Faith." Read Hebrews 11:31. How is Rahab described in this verse? How do we remember her today because of this description?

> **Meditate & Memorize:**
>
> *"Whoever sows to please their flesh, from the flesh will reap destruction; whoever sows to please the Spirit, from the Spirit will reap eternal life. Let us not become weary in doing good, for at the proper time we will reap a harvest if we do not give up."*
>
> —Galatians 6:8-9[56]

19. How is Rahab's faith like the mustard seed we read about on Day One in Matthew 13:31?

20. By becoming a follower of Jesus, acknowledging His grace as the only way to salvation, we become co-heirs with Him and citizens of His Kingdom. We then have the privilege of being used by Him for Kingdom glory.

DAY FIVE

Take some time to pray and reflect on the growth stage in your own life.

21. What are some areas you think God might like to cultivate and grow you? Make a list of some of your talents, interests, and gifts. Are you a great baker? Do you like to write encouraging notes? Are you good at researching about a certain topic and then breaking it down so it's easier for others to understand? Do you make people laugh? What are you fascinated by? Can you sit and be present with people when they are grieving? Is God calling you to invest more in your marriage or spend more quality time with your kids? Jot down some areas God might be calling you to explore in the coming season that you haven't had time for in the past.

   _____

   _____

   _____

22. Think about some activities, relationships, distractions or other things you might need to weed out of your garden to make time for growth and learning. Fill in the chart below with activities you believe God is calling you to spend less time on and those He would like you to invest in more.

LESS:	MORE:

23. Write a prayer in the space below asking God to help you on this journey to flourishing.

DAY SIX

24. Make a list of five key people in your life. This might be a spouse, friend, child or neighbor. Next to each name jot down what you see are their strengths or gifts. How has the Lord used that person in your life?

_____

_____

_____

_____

25. Brainstorm some ways you could acknowledge these strengths and gifts to them and encourage them to keep growing.

_____

_____

_____

_____

WEEK SIX
BLOOM

This past January, my husband Shawn surprised me with a 5-day anniversary trip to the Big Island of Hawaii. He cashed in on some airline miles, and we were able to stay at his sister's condo in Kona. As far as I was concerned, this was the perfect way to celebrate our first anniversary in the middle of January.

Shawn knows something in me blooms when I'm traveling. Although I have been to Hawaii several times, the Big Island was new to me. I love the adventure of discovering a new place—trying out the local eats, exploring shops and trails, and hunting down the most beautiful vistas. The Big Island did not disappoint. Probably my favorite memory was our last day on the island. We hopped in our rental car early that morning and followed the curve of the Highway 11 south to the other side of the island. We stopped at the famous Punalu'u Black Sand Beach and saw a cluster of majestic sea turtles sunbathing near the shore. God's glory danced before me in this unique landscape.

We had plans for lunch with a friend and former colleague of mine who lived in a little town on that side of the island called Ka'u. Joan and her husband Ralph chose a career change after her father died and joined her mom to manage the family coffee business. Joan told me there were no restaurants in her town. She always prepared home-cooked meals for their guests. We were happy to oblige. They welcomed us to their table with roasted chicken, sticky rice, green salad with sweet potatoes, and the most delectable pear pie from a local bakery. I can still taste the buttery crust and perfectly-sweetened fruit filling. And, of course, they served up coffee—one of the most amazing cups of coffee I've ever had in my life with notes of lime, chocolate and brown sugar.

After lunch, Joan and Ralph took us on a little tour of their coffee farm. We followed their truck up the hill a few miles and began to learn about the fascinating process of growing coffee. I had no idea of the hard work and care that goes into cultivating quality coffee beans. Rusty's Hawaiian coffee is award-winning for a reason. As ocean waves swished their hula skirts in the distance, I stood on the hillside and leaned in close to a coffee tree. Joan pointed out delicate white, jasmine-scented flowers; unripe coffee cherries; ripe coffee cherries all on the same tree. These were the varied stages of the harvest all displayed on one plant. The flowers would one day become fruit. The cherries would ripen to be picked and roasted and turned into that perfect cup of coffee. Joan said Ka'u is a unique place to grow coffee because the climate creates a longer blooming period compared to other parts of the world. The frequent rains on this side of the island can sometimes result in an eight-month harvest season.

That image of the coffee tree heavy with coffee cherries in various stages and flowers really stuck with me. I meditated on the idea that a frequent mixture of sunlight and rain produces a greater crop. The same is true in our lives. If it were all sunshine in our life gardens, we would miss the deep lessons God has for us. It's the intermittent rain, the trials of many kinds that force the blooms. And one day those blooms become the fruit ripened and ready to be picked.

In the Old Testament, the Jews gave their firstfruits as a gift to God. They were expected to bring the first part of their harvest to God's house.[52] This custom was written into their law. It was a way of expressing allegiance and gratitude to God, the giver of all things, who had rescued them out of Egypt and brought them to a land of milk and honey. In agriculture today, the firstfruits are the first produce of a season—often picked and examined to offer a foretaste of the crop that is to come.

This story goes back even further to the creation of the world. Adam and Eve betrayed God's trust by eating that forbidden fruit in the Garden. Then God, in His mercy and grace, sent His one and only Son as a sacrifice, the firstfruit to redeem humanity. 1 Corinthians 15:20-21 references this important concept comparing Christ to the firstfruits: "But in fact Christ has been raised from the dead, the firstfruits of those who have fallen asleep. For as by a man came death, by a man has come also the resurrection of the dead. For as in Adam all die, so also in Christ shall all be made alive."[53] Paul is emphasizing an important truth to the Corinthian church in this passage. He is reiterating that Jesus Christ and his resurrection from the dead is the crux of the Gospel. Christ was offered up as the firstfruits, the first sacrifice. In his death, the breaking of the seed, new life sprung forth. Each one of us is offered the gift of grace, which includes the gift of eternal life, if we accept it. Life is multiplied through Christ's death and resurrection.

Martin Luther said, "Our Lord has written the promise of resurrection, not in books alone, but in every leaf in springtime."[54] If we look around us, the whole earth declares His glory. The rose bush, the grapevine, the blooming daffodils in a spacious vase, the perennial freesia in front of my house, the tomato plant in our Chicago garden, the mustard seed growing into a tree large enough to make a home for birds—all of these speak of death and resurrection, and of flourishing. These last five weeks we have followed the process of flourishing. We contemplated what it means to *plant* and root ourselves in good soil. We pressed in to see the value in *pruning* and offering up the pruning knife to the Master Gardener so He might shape us for the greater yield. We explored the power of detoxing from our busyness and embracing soul *rest* as part of the growth process. We pursued what it means to *nourish* well and with the proper water, food and light in all seasons. We dug into methods to *cultivate* a life in Christ and be used by Him to encourage growth in others. And finally, this week we are rushing forward to see all this work in *bloom*.

This week you are invited to explore the story of Saul, who became Paul when his life was changed by Christ on the road to Damascus. His testimony and ministry swept across the entire New Testament. We do not have time to study every small detail of Saul's life, but hopefully you will consider the bird's eye view of his life garden. I am fascinated by the transformation in Saul's life. One day he was leading the brigade to persecute Christians, the next day he saw a light—literally—and the trajectory of his life is changed forever.

Saul was a young man of 20 when Jesus was crucified and resurrected. He took his first missionary journey at age 36. He was imprisoned at age 47, where he wrote his letters to the Ephesians, Philippians, Colossians, and Philemon. He was released at age 54, when he wrote 1 Timothy and Titus. Then he was imprisoned again at age 57, when he wrote 2 Timothy and was eventually martyred.[55] Meanwhile, the church was multiplying across Europe, Africa and Asia because of the way the Holy Spirit cultivated the seeds Paul planted. Paul was obedient to God and leveraged his privileges to help countless individuals and churches flourish. God used this man to multiply the Gospel message across countries and continents. Flourishing doesn't happen in isolation. Flourishing is magnified in community. Paul's life is an example of how this works. The reach, the variety of flowers and fruit, the possibilities for a flourishing garden is multiplied in community.

I have my own example of how one life can encourage growth and nourish faith in the life of another. One of the most memorable days of my life was September 13, 2014—the day of my husband Ericlee's Memorial Service. It was truly a day of celebration and storytelling as more than a thousand people packed the church. At one point, our friend Chris, who was leading the service, asked my girls, my mother-in-law and me to stand and turn around to face the audience. He wanted us to see the influence Ericlee had on our community in his 40 years of life. He asked various groups of people to stand—those Ericlee had coached, those who had ever run a race because of Ericlee, those who traveled to Haiti or participated in mission trips with Ericlee, those who attended school or church with him, those who were part of his CrossFit community, those who were his students or clients, and those he mentored and discipled. It was a powerful moment.

After the service, my girls celebrated their daddy's life by playing and jumping in bounce houses with their friends. Meanwhile, I welcomed a receiving line in the gymnasium next to the church where he had played and coached countless games. For four hours, I stood there while people came to tell me story after story of how my husband changed their lives. The most treasured stories were from students and athletes who had been challenged by Ericlee to pursue God's call and spiritual growth in their lives. I think of that day often. Ericlee took time to ask the hard questions, to encourage and to challenge people to do more than they believed they could do. I am personally inspired to live out his legacy and model it for my children.

DAY ONE

Paul is an example of a man whose life was completely transformed by Jesus Christ. He was a Pharisee who persecuted Christ-followers until one day when he had a miraculous conversion experience. Read Acts chapter 9:1-18.

1. Saul is traveling and quite literally stopped on the road. Describe what happens to him.

2. What do you think is the significance of the light in this passage?

3. Do a little research. What role does the light play in the growth and blooming of a plant?

4. According to verse 15, what task was Saul chosen for?

5. Verse 18 says that something like scales fell from Saul's eyes? Why do you think this is important to Saul's conversion story?

DAY TWO

6. After Saul sees the light and hears from Jesus, he takes action. Read about Saul's specific and bold actions in obedience to Christ in Acts 9:19-31.

7. According to Acts 9:17-20, what does Saul begin to do immediately after gaining new strength?

8. Barnabas is instrumental in helping the disciples receive Saul into their group. What does he do for Saul?

9. Put yourself in the shoes of the disciples and those hearing Saul in the synagogues. This is the man who approved of the stoning of Stephen described in Acts 7:54-8:1. How do you think you would receive his message given his past and his testimony?

10. Have you ever had the chance to introduce someone to a group you are a part of? What kinds of things did you say or do to help bring that person into the fold?

11. How does the cross make us outsiders who are invited inside?

DAY THREE

Saul's conversion experience is highlighted many times throughout the book of Acts and other times in his own writings. Let's look together at one example of Saul sharing his testimony. Read Acts 26:12-29. Keep in mind at this point Saul is talking to a mostly Gentile audience.

12. What is different about this account of Saul's conversion? How does Saul shape his testimony to reach out to his Gentile audience?

13. Describe the purpose or commissioning Saul says Jesus gave him in verse 16. What is he being called to do?

14. Earlier in Acts 23:26 it is revealed that Paul is a Roman citizen. He is protected by his citizenship. Are there other privileges or God-given gifts Paul has that he can leverage to help spread the gospel? What might he use to his advantage to help others bloom?

We are each uniquely positioned and equipped to align with His purpose for our lives.

DAY FOUR

Saul (whose name is eventually changed to Paul) is responsible for much of the writing of the New Testament. Many of the books included in the New Testament were actually letters written by Paul to the various churches he had helped cultivate. He wrote to the Romans, Corinthians, Galatians, Ephesians, Colossians, and Thessalonians, while he was in prison. He additionally writes three letters—often called the Pastoral Epistles—to Timothy and Titus.[57] Let's look together at a few of Paul's letters to see how he invested in others, encouraged them to develop spiritual fruit, and helped them to flourish.

15. In Paul's letter to the Galatians, he specifically defends salvation by faith and warns the believers in the church against abandoning the things he originally taught them. Read Galatians 5:16-26. List the Fruit of the Spirit described by Paul in Galatians 5:22.

16. These nine fruits are characteristics or behaviors which provide evidence of the Holy Spirit in believers. How does this fit with our theme of flourishing?

17. Read Galatians 6:7-10. Paul uses another agricultural metaphor in these verses. What do you think is his main message or point in these verses?

18. Keeping in mind we do not "earn" our salvation by doing good, how do these verses give you a richer understanding of what it means to flourish together?

DAY FIVE

In his book, *Making All Things New*, R. York Moore talks about a future vision and God's dream for our future and the earth. He writes, "God's dream is to make all things new in a way that causes all the earth, every people and every thing to flourish to the glory of God."[58]

19. How do you respond to this quote?

20. Read Revelation 22:1-5. This passage of scripture gives us a picture of flourishing and the restoration of Eden that God promises in the future. Make a list or draw a picture of some of things described here that will be restored.

21. What are some other things you imagine will be repaired and restored in the future? Think about injustices reversed, relationships repaired, damage to the earth restored, etc. Describe how you envision our world in its true state of flourishing.

22. What is your response? How does longing for Heaven impact you today?

_____

_____

_____

_____

_____

We can experience restoration today through Jesus Christ, although not fully until we are with Him in eternity.

DAY SIX

23. Get out a highlighter. Thumb through this Bible study workbook. Highlight some of the points or discoveries that have made an impact on you. Jot down at least three of those points below.

24. How will this study impact your faith journey moving forward? What will you take away or do as a result of what you have learned?

DEAR LEADER FRIENDS

I am so humbled and grateful for you willingness to join me on this journey of learning to flourish together. As a facilitator of this Bible study, you have a special opportunity to encourage and lead others into a deeper understanding and relationship with Jesus Christ.

Some of the activities in this study may challenge your group. They might have to step out of their comfort zones to draw a picture or journal a reflection or write a prayer. I hope you will model this for them by being vulnerable. I encourage you to **take the first step** *and invite them to come along.*

Get to know the people in your group. *Where are they coming from? Where are they in their faith journey? My desire is that women who feel parched and disconnected from the Vine will reconnect with God through this study.*

If you are taking time to discuss the homework in your groups, do not feel like you need to cover every question. **Highlight a few of the questions to dig deeper.** *Give the women time to respond thoughtfully and apply the questions to their current contexts.*

When you find that women have not had time to complete the homework, **offer them grace.** *There are all kinds of reasons people cannot get to the homework. Continue to encourage them to carve out the daily time to complete the study. You might want to read the passages aloud in your group and then answer the questions together to help guide the group members to deeper understanding.*

*I also want to encourage you to **take time to cover the memory verses** each week. You might suggest the women write these out and read them or recite them aloud when you are together. Many believe they are not good at memorizing but some encouragement from you goes a long way to helping them learn God's Word.*

***Be creative.** Make this study your own. You might consider concluding with a special activity like a Garden Party. Groups could arrange succulents in pots or do a service project together, like planting flowers for a local school or widow in your group.*

*I am praying over each one of you as you dig in to cultivate a more fruitful life in Christ. Thank you for partnering with me in the Gospel. Please **do not hesitate to reach out** to me with comments or questions. You can email me at dorina@dorinagilmore.com.*

For His Glory,
Dorina

END NOTES

INTRODUCTION

1. Merriam-Webster Online, "flourish," Accessed February 10, 2017, https://www.merriam-webster.com/dictionary/flourish.
2. Andy Crouch, *Strong and Weak: Embracing A Life Of Love, Risk and True Flourishing*. (Downer's Grove: InterVarsity Press, 2016) 11.
3. John 15: 2-3, English Standard Version.
4. John 4:13-14, English Standard Version.
5. Margaret Feinberg, *Flourish: Live loved. Live fearless. Live free.* (Franklin: Worthy, 2016) 178.
6. John 15:8, English Standard Version.

WEEK ONE—PLANT

7. Isaiah 43:19, English Standard Version.
8. Ann Voskamp, *The Broken Way: A Daring Path Into the Abundant Life*. (Grand Rapids, Zondervan, 2016), 26.
9. Jeremiah 17:7-8, New Living Translation.
10. John 7:38, English Standard Version.
11. William Morgan, "An Overview of the Plant Lifecycles." The North American Farmer blog https://northamericanfarmer.com/science/life-cycle-of-a-plant/ (Accessed November 1, 2017).
12. Ephesians 2:8-10, New Living Translation
13. Memory Verse: Jeremiah 17:7-8, New Living Translation

WEEK TWO—PRUNE

14. John 15:3-4, The Message.
15. David Roper, "The Pruning," *A Burden Shared. (Grand Rapids: Discovery House Publishers, 1991) 95-96.*
16. Bible Hub, "prune," Accessed February 21, 2017, http://biblehub.com/topical/p/prune.htm.
17. Andy Crouch, *Strong and Weak: Embracing A Life Of Love, Risk and True Flourishing.* (Downer's Grove: InterVarsity Press, 2016) 11.
18. David Roper, "The Pruning," *A Burden Shared. (Grand Rapids: Discovery House Publishers,* 1991*) 95-96.*
19. Memory Verse: John 15:1-2, English Standard Version.
20. Dorothy Kelley Patterson, general editor. "The Book of John." *The Study Bible for Women. Holman Christian Standard Bible* (Nashville: Holman Bible Publishers, 2014), 1370-1371.
21. John 15: 1-17, English Standard Version
22. Dorothy Kelley Patterson, general editor. "The Book of Genesis." *The Study Bible for Women. Holman Christian Standard Bible* (Nashville: Holman Bible Publishers, 2014), 3.
23. Hebrews 12:6, English Standard Version
24. Romans 8:32, New International Version
25. Shauna Niequist, "*Present Over Perfect: Leaving Behind Frantic For a Simpler, more Soulful Way of Living*" (Grand Rapids: Zondervan, 2016) 200.

WEEK THREE—REST

26. Matthew 11:28-30, New Living Translation.
27. Margaret Feinberg, *Flourish: Live loved. Live fearless. Live free.* (Franklin: Worthy, 2016) 166.
28. Genesis 2:1-3, Holman Christian Standard Bible.
29. Dorothy Kelley Patterson, general editor. "The Book of Psalms." *The Study Bible for Women. Holman Christian Standard Bible* (Nashville: Holman Bible Publishers, 2014), 669.
30. Mark 6:31-32, New Living Translation.
31. Psalm 127:2, English Standard Version.

32. Rebecca Lyons, *You Are Free: Be Who You Already Are*. (Grand Rapids: Zondervan, 2017), 141.
33. Psalm 46:10, English Standard Version.
34. Margaret Feinberg, *Flourish: Live loved. Live fearless. Live free.* (Franklin: Worthy, 2016) 154-155.
35. Matthew 11:28, English Standard Version.
36. Matthew 11:28-30, The Message.
37. Sherry Harney, *Twelve Women of the Bible: Life-Changing Stories For Women Today*. (Grand Rapids: Zondervan, 2010) 108.
38. Jennie Allen, *Nothing to Prove: Why We Can Stop Trying So Hard*. (New York: Waterbrook, 2017), 138.

WEEK FOUR—NOURISH

39. Merriam-Webster Dictionary, "perennial," Accessed March 22, 2017. https://www.merriam-webster.com/dictionary/perennial.
40. Ecclesiastes 1:1, New International Version.
41. Matthew 11:28-30, The Message.
42. 1 Corinthians 6:19-20, New Living Translation.
43. John 6:35, Holman Christian Standard Bible.
44. John 4:13-14, Holman Christian Standard Bible.
45. Jennie Allen, *Nothing to Prove: Why We Can Stop Trying So Hard*. (New York: Waterbrook, 2017), 217.
46. John 7:37, Holman Christian Standard Bible.
47. 2 Corinthians 4:6, New International Version.
48. Isaiah 55:10-11, New International Version.
49. Ann Voskamp, *The Broken Way: A Daring Path Into the Abundant Life*. (Grand Rapids, Zondervan, 2016), 199.
50. Ann Voskamp, *The Broken Way: A Daring Path Into the Abundant Life*. (Grand Rapids, Zondervan, 2016), 207.

WEEK FIVE—CULTIVATE

51. Merriam-Webster Dictionary, "cultivate," Accessed May 2, 2017. https://www.merriam-webster.com/dictionary/cultivate.
52. Mark Batterson, "The Power of a Single Seed," *Mount Hermon Christian Writer's Conference*, April 9, 2017.
53. Isaiah 61:11, New International Version.
54. Matthew 17:20, New International Version.
55. Annie Downs, *Let's All Be Brave: Living Life With Everything You Have.* (Grand Rapids, Zondervan, 2014), 89.
56. Matthew 13:31-32, Holman Christian Standard Bible.
57. Dorothy Kelley Patterson, general editor. "The Book of Matthew." *The Study Bible for Women. Holman Christian Standard Bible* (Nashville: Holman Bible Publishers, 2014), 1262.
58. Dorothy Kelley Patterson, general editor. "The Book of Joshua." *The Study Bible for Women. Holman Christian Standard Bible* (Nashville: Holman Bible Publishers, 2014), 254.
59. Dorothy Kelley Patterson, general editor. "The Book of Joshua." *The Study Bible for Women. Holman Christian Standard Bible* (Nashville: Holman Bible Publishers, 2014), 256.
60. Isaiah 53:5, New International Version.

WEEK SIX—BLOOM

61. See Deuteronomy 26: 2-11.
62. 1 Corinthians 15:20-21, English Standard Version.
63. Martin Luther quoted in "May 21-27 section." Jenn Giles Kemper, editor. *Sacred Ordinary Days Liturgical Planner*, 2005.
64. Angie Smith, *Seamless*. (Nashville: LifeWay, 2015), 145.
65. Galatians 6:8-9, New International Version.
66. Dorothy Kelley Patterson, general editor. "The Book of 1 Timothy." *The Study Bible for Women. Holman Christian Standard Bible* (Nashville: Holman Bible Publishers, 2014), 1542.
67. R. York Moore, *Making All Things New: God's Dream for Global Justice.* (Downers Grove, InterVarsity Press, 2012), 152.

ACKNOWLEDGEMENTS

I started writing *Flourishing Together* in early 2017. As God was teaching me the steps to flourish by His design, I began to take notes. I realized many of my close friends were trying to find their way on a similar journey. I lived this message, and I knew I needed to share it with others.

To my husband Shawn Young, who inspired and championed this project from start to finish. You offered a keen editing eye, a sound business mind and a sacrificial love that I needed to follow this project to completion. Thank you for investing in me daily!

To my three daughters, Meilani, Giada and Zayla, who cheered me on every step of the way. Thank you for your grace when I was writing and editing in every crack of time I could find.

To my parents Doug and Maria Lazo, who have encouraged my writing since I was in grade school. Thanks, Mom, for always being an honest editor and a relentless cheerleader. To my mother-in-law Christene, who gave her time to help watch my kids so I could write.

To the first Flourishing Together group, my heart friends, Stacie Benedict, Cori Schmidt, and Heather Fenton, who received the "down draft" of this project with such grace. Thank you for digging in with me to envision and cultivate this project.

ACKNOWLEDGEMENTS

To my editing friends, Jenny Gorans, Kathy Moore, Emily Allen, Carlene Seghers, and Kristin Vanderlip, who offered up helpful suggestions and abundant support for this project. I am forever grateful for your time and investment.

To my Go Mama Workout friends, who prayed me through and embraced the message of this study.

To the others in my community, including Troy and Allison Vasquez, Michael Fenton, Forest Benedict, Darrel Schmidt, Whitney Bunker, Melissa Danisi, Beth Nicoletto, Sybil Kolbert and many others, who offered support on the journey.

To my Chai sisters, Amy Tosland, Terry Rios, Yasmin Rodrigues and Carla Reyes-Cuerva, who walk with me through every year's "one word" theme.

To all my Hope*Writer friends, who have provided inspiration, support, editing help, encouragement and so much more!

Made in the USA
Columbia, SC
03 January 2019